Miss Elvester, Mary W. Paxton

Miss Elvester's Girls

Vol. 1

Miss Elvester, Mary W. Paxton

Miss Elvester's Girls
Vol. 1

ISBN/EAN: 9783337346386

Printed in Europe, USA, Canada, Australia, Japan

Cover: Foto ©Thomas Meinert / pixelio.de

More available books at **www.hansebooks.com**

MISS ELVESTER'S GIRLS.

A NOVEL.

BY

THE AUTHOR OF 'BY-WAYS.'

IN THREE VOLUMES.

VOL. I.

LONDON: TINSLEY BROTHERS,
8 CATHERINE STREET, STRAND, W.C.

1 8 8 3.

COLSTON AND SON, PRINTERS, EDINBURGH.

CONTENTS.

CHAPTER VIII.

MISS ELVESTER'S GIRLS.

PROLOGUE.

THERE is a world of difference between Shetland, when her skies are lovely, her waters are flashing in the sunlight, her hillocks and hollows are aglow with vivid flowers; and Shetland, when the mantle she wears is dun, and the heavens lour gloomily, and every loch and creek and voe gives back the frown. She is in this latter condition the day when I ask you to take your stand with me for a moment on a certain mossy height, unknown to geographers, but called

by the dwellers beside it, Vostaberg
Knowe.

From our observatory we look over to
the village of Bresta, two or three score
cottages and cots of primitive design, scattered in semi-circular fashion about the head
of a miniature bay.   Yonder, marked out
by their respective sign-boards, are the estab-
lishments of merchants (by ' merchant ' is to
be understood, in strict literalness, a dealer
in everything, ' from a needle to an anchor '),
baker—no butcher, alas !—grocer, ' Licensed
in Spirits and Ales,' and post-mistress, with
whom lodges the doctor, when doctor there
chances to be.   Those houses, larger and
of a different class from the rest, we guess
to be manses ; and small as the village is,
there are no fewer than four churches
within its borders.   We judge, therefore,
that its people must have theology enough,
whatever else they lack.

It is mail-day, and the letter-carrier, hours
too late in arriving (that is nothing in Shetland), now rests in glory after his thirty

miles' walk from the capital. He is the most important person in the village, for the nonce; he is the weekly newspaper.

The various groups gathered round the post-office form a picturesque whole; storm-tanned fishermen who know Greenland waters well; lads who have not yet been farther than 'The Haaf'; old crones profuse of pious speech, which daily life as often as not belies; younger matrons, nearly as weather - worn as the men; and girls, with fine free carriage, and blue or scarlet kerchief shading faces as bonny—many of them—as faces need to be. Besides these, there are the parish clergyman, handsome, bronzed, and bearded, towering Saul-like above the people; the doctor, a jovial young fellow, who came to Shetland in a sort of frolic some months ago, and freely owns himself more than a trifle tired of his diversion now; the Independent pastor's son, riding a saddleless sheltie and grasping the mane for reins; the Free Kirk schoolmaster's maid-of-all-works, diligently applying herself to newsmonging; and, to finish the list pleasingly, the Methodist minister's young wife, lately transplanted from amidst Kentish hop-gardens, but wonderfully happy, if appearances are to be trusted, despite the change.

Many letters fell to this lady's share, and she gaily remarked to the parish clergyman, as together they left the post-office,—

'You see I've got my basket quite full, Mr Berwick. There is this advantage about receiving letters only once a-week, that we get such a number at a time.'

Mr Berwick was not so fond of letters as Mrs Rich, and could not be very enthusiastic on the subject. However, he did his best, and said,—

'And but one disappointment in the week should an expected letter fail to come.'

'Indeed, yes; that is a mercy too. The only thing to grumble over, is the being kept waiting for one's budget so very, very long after it has reached the island.'

'The remedy for which,' said Mr Berwick,

'is a mail-bag of your own and a special messenger.'

' I daresay, but unless you are the master of Eastravoe, for instance, you can't afford such luxuries. The girls at Eastravoe— favoured of fortune that they are !— will have read all their love-letters hours ago.'

' Hours ago!' echoed Mr Berwick. And then he bade his companion notice how creamy Bresta Sound was, and how yon inky clouds had blotted out the distant Fitful Head.

' You're weatherwise,' said she, smiling to herself, however, at his abrupt change of theme ; ' shall we have it rough to-night?'

' Won't we!' he rejoined. ' This evening's steamer will enjoy a rare toss in Sumburgh Roost. Be glad you are not to be on board, Mrs Rich.'

' It isn't to be another of your great storms, I hope ? '

' But you don't know anything about our great storms, as yet.'

'No?   What is it that you call a great storm, please?'

'It is when my stable roof is lifted clean off, and when going out to see what's likely to happen next, I am forced to lie flat on the ground to escape being blown over the hills like thistledown.'

'You blown over the hills like thistle-down!' she laughed; 'a very odd kind of thistledown, indeed.'

So they went on talking till the Methodist manse was reached.   Here Mr Berwick shook hands with a gentleman who came to the front garden gate.

'You have learnt Shetland manners to some purpose,' he observed; 'Mrs Rich bears the burden; you look on.'

'Mrs Rich is very willing to be burdened so,' said Mrs Rich's husband.

'Sorry is the plight of him who has no excuse ready!' exclaimed the other, laughing. 'On first coming to Bresta, I was full of schemes for the reformation of the island. Well, one day a woman toiled from Scullo-

way with a box of books for me, her lord
following her to the manse for the payment.
I told him rather hotly what I thought about
setting women to men's work, though I know
I might quite as well have held my peace.
They defend the usage, these Shetland hus-
bands ; they have " Scripture for't,' and refer
you to chapter and verse in Nehemiah,
where it is written :—" And next unto him
repaired Shallum the son of Halokesh, the
ruler of the half part of Jerusalem, he and
his *daughters*." But I must not keep you
longer from your letters, Mrs Rich ; and I
expect both your husband and I will find
among ours several of those interesting
communications which demand an immediate
answer.'

' Oh, I know the kind ; they are addressed
in that ugly scrawl which students cultivate.
Talk of a lady's hand being hard to read !
It is print compared to a minister's. I—excuse me, Mr Berwick, and you, Arthur—I
don't like ministerial communications at all.'

' Candidly speaking, I don't either, Mrs

Rich ; for if they be not claiming your fulfilment of some hazy half promise to give an address at the writer's forthcoming congregational soiree, they are to excuse the writer for breaking his word about *your* congregational soiree ; he has caught a cold, and must shun night air. *P.S.*—He reminds you of his Fast-day, and, in the present state of the roads, would advise you not to risk the short-cut, but to take the extra ten miles and the ferry.'

And having thus outdone Mrs Rich in disparagement of clerical correspondence, the Rev. Donald Berwick, Bachelor of Divinity, set his face homewards. He went so far along the margin of the sound, then struck off to the right, and ascended Vostaberg Knowe, from the top of which, across an undulating grassy stretch of scattald or common, strewn with stones, studded with rough, grey boulders, and pastured on by shaggy ponies, the parish manse could be seen. It was a big, plain, substantial house, just like any other Scotch parsonage. It had an extensive glebe attached; a little fresh-water loch lay behind, and to the front spread a grand panorama of the open sea. From village to manse measured about a mile; but the way lay over the pathless scattald, therefore if you, a stranger, should attempt that distance alone and afoot on any misty day, all the chances were, that you would hopelessly wander, though, before setting out, you had laughed to scorn the very notion of losing yourself *there*, were the day ever so misty.

Near his own house, Mr Berwick was overtaken by one who had been shouting after him in vain, while he, never turning his head, had continued his quick march across the scattald.

'What, you, Gledcairny!' he exclaimed, on looking about and seeing that he who had laid hold of him with so ungentle a grip was the young doctor, whom he had left in the post-office.

'Yes, I, Gledcairny,' said his captor. 'Didst not hear my cry?'

'No; or if I did, took it for a sea-mew's.'

'Some fellows have no sense of the musical; but I forgive you, and will be at your place to-night to see if any of the master of Eastravoe's cigars are left.'

'All right.'

'I don't know about its being all right; for, fine specimen as I am, never a box of cigars is sent to me. Is it any fault of mine that I'm not a Cornrigshire man, or any merit of yours that you are?'

'Who says it is?'

'Whether they say so or not, that's what our autocrat of Eastravoe and his daughters think. The master's first wife, as everybody knows, was one of the Cornrigshire Mearnsmuirs.'

'And I come of a stock of Cornrigshire farmers. Yes, the connection is striking and clear.'

'They are nice girls, those Elvesters (you swear to the fact, and you should know),' pursued the doctor argumentatively; 'but it would do them a high mountain of good, just to be shaken out of this corner where every soul is subject to them, and set down in a part of the world where somebody else is supreme, and where they would be made to see their own real importance. They want to have it demonstrated to them that they've fallen into a little mistake in thinking themselves princesses.'

'So they are princesses in Shetland.'

'Ay, that is it—in Shetland; but what would they be anywhere else?'

'Still Shetland princesses,' said Mr Berwick, and being now at the manse gate, he invited his friend to enter.

But Mr Gledcairny was on his way to vaccinate a batch of babies.

'And the thrice unblessed post,' said he, 'has detained me too long already. It will be good luck if I'm not belated in the wilds this night, and swallowed by a peat bog, or blown over a cliff, to have my elegy chanted by the sea-fowls.'

'Carry the Shetlander's torch, a blazing peat! I'll send you a pair of tongs,' said Mr

Berwick. 'No? Well, then, accept some
patient's hospitality for the night.'

'I don't call myself fastidious—not very;
only there is a limit to all things. But whom
in the region of Giersness would you recom-
mend as a hostess, say you?'

'Cheyne Ollason; she will bring the tea-
pot from among her bedclothes to refresh
you withal.'

Dr Gledcairny grinned.

'I know all about that,' he replied;
'Mother Ollason is a fast friend of mine.
Poor soul, she nearly yielded up the ghost
when she heard that you had been seen
skating on your loch down there; and she
has been quaking ever since, through fear
that "a skating minister canna, canna be
a fitting guide to heaven."'

'I wish skating were the worst of me,'
was the response.

Then these two professional men parted
as unceremoniously as they had met, and
the one went up to his door, the other on
to his business.

The study into which Mr Berwick took
his way was lined round and round with
books ; packed with pamphlets and maga-
zines, and rich in manuscripts; indeed, if
the truth must be spoken, it was a place
to make any methodical woman's fingers
fairly tingle. However, its owner saw
nothing amiss with his room. It suited
him ; everything lay just where he could
put his hand on it ; there were no nonsensi-
calities about to stumble over and make you
' Curse that stool !' What then would man
want more ? And it was all right, to be
sure, seeing the man in question had only
himself to please. As he was in the act of
taking a seat to look at what he had brought
from the post-office, something in the letter-
rack over the mantelpiece caught his eye.
He drew it out, and standing before the fire
(the great heat of which probably accounted
for the sudden access of colour to his face),
broke the seal, and read :—

' DEAR MR BERWICK,—Kindly oblige me

by coming to Eastravoe as soon as you con-
veniently can.   My father is in great trouble,
and there is no one within reach except
yourself to whom he will speak of his
affairs.—I am, very sincerely yours,

' JANET MEARNSMUIR ELVESTER.'

Other letters, demanded they immediate
answer or not, got none of Mr Berwick's
attention that day.   He rang the bell.   Immediately stood a red-cheeked, bright-eyed
little elderly woman in the doorway, with a—-

' Please, sir, an' what wanted you ? '

' Bid Magnus catch and saddle the Howlet,'
said Mr Berwick.

' And a storm coming on so surely !' she
ejaculated.   ' It canna be.'

That meant nothing, however.   To say
things could not be, was merely a habit the
housekeeper had got.

' Peery (little) Peter O'Haavra is at the
back-door even now,' she went on to inform
her master.   ' Would you be pleased to see
him, Mr Berwick ? '

She pronounced the name as Shetlanders pronounce that of their principal town, sounding the *w*. Nor did the minister object: on the contrary, used to hear himself called so by certain pretty lips secretly dear to him, he had come to think that ' Berrick ' was disagreeably harsh.

' What should I see the laddie for ? ' he asked. ' What's wanted to-day ? '

' He has fetched a gran' ling fish,—a present, sir.'

Mr Berwick abominated ling fish, and presents no less. He knew what a Shetland present meant, so—

' How much, Barbara ? ' he inquired.

' I donna ken, I'm sure,' returned Barbara demurely ; ' just what you please, sir.'

' There,' said this unthankful recipient of ling fish, taking a florin from his purse, ' give that to peery Peter, and tell him that he needn't mind to bring any more presents for a while to come.'

As she stepped forward to take the coin, Barbara inquired,—

'Please, got you yon letter Olaf brocht, sir?'

'Yes, yes; I have seen it.'

'That is affa bad news for the master, and—'

'My good Barbara, let news alone, and attend to your proper business — which is, just now, the Howlet.'

'I canna help the news, sir; there is always a good deal o' people comes this airt. And Lily o' Runigarth was saying—'

'No matter what. Spare me Lily of Runigarth's gossip.'

'Vera weel, sir. She was only asking would the minister be for Hilyascord to-day. That's great ongauns at Hilyascord, Mr Berwick.'

'The minister will not be for Hilyascord to-day. I am going to Eastravoe—and immediately, if it were possible to get away.'

'And ging you to Eastravoe fasting, Mr Berwick? It canna be. Shall I fetch—'

'Nothing whatever. Am I to see the Howlet this afternoon?'

'*Ja, ja*, that'll you; he is none so far off
—just roun' by the raddle, sir. But yon is
the langsome ride, it is, and the blawy! And
the verra last minister o' Bresta, he was
sic' like's yoursel', Mr Berwick; no thocht
o' refreshments would he take, nor no muffler
would he put on. Weel, sir, mony came
the Sabbath days when he couldna, couldna
preach, poor gentleman, coughing he was so
bitterly. Never was a wearier cough as his,
neither in Shetland nor Great Britain, sir.'

Impatient as he was, Mr Berwick could
not forbear laughing.

'Shetland or Great Britain!' he echoed.
'And what may your notion of Great Britain
be, Barbara?'

'I donna like yon place, sir; it is a' hooses
—hooses, an' where it isna hooses it is trees.
I couldna bide that, Mr Berwick; I would pine
an' think lang for the free Shetland hills.'

Then, her own time being come, Barbara
went to send Magnus to catch the Howlet;
and soon after, her master, mounted on a
handsome black fetlar, set out for Eastravoe.

In this direction there *was* a road, and, with stray exceptions, a pretty passable one —something to be thankful for in Shetland. On the right hand lay a plain, bounded by a multitude of little hills, with peat mosses below, and many a tarn between, lighted into momentary ruby by the setting sun; for the sun had half withdrawn the curtains of his cloud-tent, and was flushing with an angry crimson all the western heavens. On the left the sward grew smoothly unbroken, save where the headland had been scalped by the peasantry for fuel, to the very lip of the precipice which overhung the German Ocean. It was spring-tide, and a strong swell stirred the sea. Here was a very magnificence of breakers! Deep was calling unto deep,— reverberating within mysterious rock caverns. —swinging bewilderingly round fantastic cliff-columns, that stood up out of all the foam and fury like grim sentinels on guard,—and filling the whole space between earth and sky with a great and mighty roar. It was an impressive sight; one to make you shrink, perhaps, and pray for the speedy shelter of comfortable curtained rooms ; or else, if you had in you anything responsive to nature's wilder moods, to set your pulses throbbing, to blind your eyes with tears, you could not tell for what, to steep you in an overpowering sense of your own littleness.

Shortly after sundown was reached the half-way point between the manse of Bresta and the house of Eastravoe,—a hamlet called Stappensting, Mr Berwick dismounted before one of the dwellings (one was a facsimile of all), a rudely constructed stone hut, enclosed within a low fence formed of 'divots' of turf. Having vainly knocked, he lifted the latch and looked in. The German tenant was not at home, but tenants of other species were ; to wit, a sheep, a pig, and an assortment of fowls, perched wherever they could find a roosting-place. A turf fire smouldered near the middle of the floor, and an opening overhead served the double purpose of chimney and window. A heap of peat and 'feal' (dried turf) was piled up in one corner ; an

arrangement which you dimly descried to be
a bed, occupied another, and a heterogeneous
jumble impossible to describe lay littered round
your feet. The clergyman of Bresta had
sometime since got over such sentimentalism
as shuddering dismay in viewing interiors
like this (only, on Sundays when dazzled by
the gay garden of bonnets clustered about
his pulpit in full choir, he would once in a
way think of these miserable cabins dense
with peat-reek, and would wonder), so he
wasted no time in moralising, but put the
letter, which he had volunteered to deliver,
where it would be found by the hut-holder
on her return, and resumed his solitary way.

As the darkness gathered the storm came
on in earnest ; and when rain began to fall,
the rider, to save several miles, forsook the
road and plunged boldly into a marshy track-
less waste. He did not know his way
through, nor would he so much as attempt
to find it; that was the pony's business,
not the man's. The Howlet took her
own course, accordingly ; and, thanks to her

sure-footedness and instinctive perception of locality, she and her master in due season stood safely within the great arched gateway of Eastravoe.

The house of Eastravoe was a triumph of solid masonry, as standing where it stood (on a plateau above the voe from which it took its name), and looking where it looked (through the giant rock portals of that voe —the stacks of Eastravoe—on the Northern Ocean), it had pressing need to be. All the powers of the air seemed to have broken loose about it when the minister of Bresta arrived. The rain was lashing it; the wind was howling frantically round the turrets of it; the voe was boiling like a witch's cauldron underneath. But what did that matter? No harm would come to it; for it was founded upon a rock.

The servant who admitted Mr Berwick ushered him at once into Miss Elvester's parlour, where there was no light but that of the flickering fire. A lady came through the shadows and held out her hand.

'This is a wild evening,' she said, and her voice was a singularly pleasant contralto; 'but I am speaking to no carpet-knight, so I don't apologise for having made you face the storm. You know the distress? You have read the newspaper accounts?'

'I saw your note before I had looked at the newspapers,' he replied, 'and I was not likely to stop to examine them then. Is anything seriously wrong?'

'It is only that we are ruined, Mr Berwick,' was the perfectly quiet response.

'Miss Elvester!' he cried.

'Yes; it is strange to think of,' she said, 'but none the less true for that. The Great Western Iron Company has failed, and my father is one of the largest shareholders—unlimited liability, unfortunately—read this, and this, and I think you will see that in calling it ruin I don't overstate the case.'

He read as requested, and soon became convinced that there had been no overstatement; that the case was in very deed as bad as it could be. He turned from letters and papers with a face full of the deepest concern, and,—

'You will have legal advice at once,' he said, oblivious of circumstances.

Miss Elvester recalled him to facts.

'You forget where we are,' she rejoined; 'our one steamer in the week, our present want of telegraphic communication with the south. Nor have we of Eastravoe any Leander to swim so far for love of us—and to lose his life in the venture, rash man.'

Though Donald Berwick was quite aware that this lady differed in some respects from the other women of his acquaintance, it jarred upon him when she made such a speech. If she were utterly distracted, it would be only natural. But to jest thus! As if devising the thought, Miss Elvester said,—

'I am perfectly calm, you perceive; I leave the hysteria to my sisters; there will be enough and to spare of that on their return. They are at Hilyascord this week, in happy ignorance of what awaits them. My poor girls!'

As she uttered the last three words her voice shook ; and during the ensuing silence, Mr Berwick felt—he could not see—that she was having a struggle to retain the calmness of which she had just boasted. But he dared not say a syllable. He had not here the kind of person upon whom could be lavished any of the usual sympathetic 'chaff well meant for grain.' Frank as Miss Elvester was, a man might not come quite near to her ; never near enough, certainly, to venture upon the common-places of condolence. Mr Berwick held his peace, therefore, and waited till she again should speak. Very soon she recovered herself.

'You are a favourite with my father,' she said; 'when he will see no other stranger he will see you. He is in the library now, and I am hoping it may do him good to have a talk with you. Will you see him at once, Mr Berwick ? or would you rather wait until you shall have rested a while and dined ?'

Till he should have rested and dined ! Most certainly not. He would go to her father at once. So she led the way to the library.

Light enough was in that room. Soft radiance, streaming from antique candelabra upon a white-haired man, who sat bent and motionless among his books. His face was hidden on his crossed arms, and these rested on the writing-table in front of him. The door opened and closed again, but the master did not raise his head.

'Father,' cried Miss Elvester cheerfully, 'here is Mr Berwick at last; you've been a little impatient for his coming, have you not?'

There being no answer, she went up to him and leant over his shoulder, at the same time laying her hand upon one of his. Suddenly she started back, uttered something between a sob and a cry for help, and staggered against the wall for support.

The master of Eastravoe's silence was the silence of death.

CHAPTER I.

THE SWEET USES OF ADVERSITY.

Daughter of Jove, relentless power,
Thou tamer of the human breast,
Whose iron scourge and torturing power
The bad affrights afflicts the best.

ON a certain midsummer evening early in the seventies, there was great commotion within Royal Street Railway Station, Royal Square, Netherlaw. The Fair week had come —that annual opportunity for the working-man to go at large and enjoy himself; so here the working-man was, swarming the platform, he with his womankind.

What a medley! what jostling and laughing and declaiming! what gallantly plumed hats and flower-garlanded rainbow-ribboned bonnets! what bugle - spangled jackets and costumes of the period!

In the crowd of holiday-makers, but not of it, one stood patiently — or impatiently perhaps—awaiting the train from the north. She was quite past youth, but straight as a dart, and light of motion as a girl. Having once looked at her pale, resolute face, you were sure to wander back to it again and again; sure, also, to make up your mind that it was too sarcastic in expression to be altogether pleasing. This woman owed nothing of her dignity to the dress she wore; and it must have been this austerity of attire which gave licence to a heavily-freighted porter, whose course she happened to be unconsciously obstructing, to bawl,—

'Watch yoursel', there! Get out of the way, my dear.' Instead of getting out of the way, the obstructionist turned full on the speaker's face a pair of large grey eyes, keenly bright as those of a falcon. The man saw his mistake; this was a person

accustomed not to be commanded, but to
command; so he muttered something supposed to be an apology, and made a circuit
to avoid displacing her whom he had the
moment before so unceremoniously ordered
to give way to him.   In doing this, he came
into collision with a pair of by-standing
matrons; and these took him sharply to task
for his clumsiness.   He retorted in kind.
One of the women thereupon gave him
to understand that neither for him nor his
betters would *she* listen to 'the language of
Ashdod;' counter-checks quarrelsome were
bandied; and finally the porter proceeded on
his way, with hard thoughts of all Eve's
daughters in his heart.

The objector to 'the language of Ashdod'
was a woman of a comely countenance; but
her voice, eyes, and tongue vied each with
the other in sharpness.   And her temper
was much ruffled to-day, for she had in
custody there bundles of inconvenient bulk
and unhandy shape, which were in constant
peril of falling away from her and being

trodden under foot by a mob, alike regardless and unmannerly. Her companion in
travel was a heavy-faced sallow slip of a
creature; and she too was hard bestead—
though not with bundles: a quartette of
boys of tender years hung about her skirts,
and in turn gnawed unripe apples, strove
every one with his brother, and whimpered
up and down unmusical chromatic scales of
inquiry, whether they would be 'sune aff
to the saut watter noo?'

Presently the father of these pretty ones
came along. He was a small, wisp-like
mortal, hazy and irresolute; and his undulating gait betrayed a heart merry with
—wine, let us say. Onward he moved,
with what was meant for a beam of dis-
arming fascination in his eye, but what—
so will men's best intentions fail of their
mark!—appeared to the public only a foolish
leer. Hard by his liege lady's side he
swerved from his equilibrium, and to regain
the same, clutched at the most convenient
object, which chanced to be the black-

draped figure already made mention of.
But he was doomed to woe. The hoped-
for prop eluded him, and behold! he buffeted
the air—he bit the dust.   The children,
shrieking, spurned him from their path ;
the mother crossly bade them, 'Wheesht,
ye sorrows, wheesht!' and bent a grue-
some visage on the sire ; the man stumbled
up again, raising his testimony the while
against 'thae rough, unchancy roads, ye
see, that winna let folk keep their feet the
day ava.'

The train from the north being now in
sight, she who waited for it did not stay
to hear what sympathy the victim of unchancy roads should receive from his spouse,
but advanced to meet the passengers as
they descended.   After a moment her face
became tinged with colour, and a dawning
smile brought to view a pair of unsuspected
dimples.   You were obliged to reconsider
your former decision now, and at the very
least to admit that the lady looked far more
attractive than you could have imagined,

while you had only beheld her features in
repose.

Two girls had alighted, and were gazing
inquiringly this way and that. Pale and
weary they were, and not a little bewildered
by this great and noisy crowd. But in
half a minute their sister was holding a
hand of each, and saying,—

'Let me know the worst. How many
of their properties have my clever girls
contrived to lose by the way?'

'We have lost nothing, Jenny—except our
patience,' replied the younger, whose sweet,
pure voice had that faintest, prettiest suspicion
of a foreign accent that Shetland voices have.

'And *this* is Netherlaw!' exclaimed the
other, precisely as she might, had she been
a Russian exile, have exclaimed, '*This* is
Siberia!'

'*This* is Netherlaw,' was the reply. 'It
is a gala time here, I must tell you, and
the people are dressed up to the occasion.
Just make a study of the fashions, will you,
while I see to the luggage.'

The spot selected by the girls from which to make their study chanced to be as nearly as possible that on which Miss Elvester had stood watching for the train. And the owner of the erring husband was now, heedless who might hear, putting the pointed question,—

' Is there ony ane haet i' the worl' you're fit for, Geordie Choppin ?'

As George Choppin seemed to have no idea on the subject, his wife's friend answered in his stead, saying,—

' Geordie's a thocht like oor ane, gey an' guid at haudin' up the door-cheeks.'

And from the tone in which she made the parallel, one felt fully sure that the man whom she claimed as hers, would not be permitted to uphold his door-posts unreproved.

' Na, but isna this gran' weather for the craps ?' observed the culprit, thinking perhaps to give conversation a less personal turn.

But Mrs Choppin was not interested in

the crops, and the levity of Mr Choppin's mind, as evidenced by his remark, had the effect of provoking an even wintrier frown than before, and the peevish exclamation,—

'Haud your tongue, ye angersome, drouthy, feckless little loon that ye are! Was there ever the like o' ye ken't?'

'Ay, Betty,' said the neighbour; 'I trow there's a hantle mair o' the same crabs whaur he comes frae.'

But Mr Choppin muttered,—

'I weel ken I was founded for a muckle chiel, but I sticket in the grouth,' for he tipsily resented the allusion to his outer man, though he cared nothing for the slur cast on his character.

'Sticket in the grouth, quo' he!' sneered his consort. 'Aweel, aweel; it's no been for stint o' guid leevin'; for scrimp wha may, I ken *ane* maun aye pick an' pree the best.'

'*I* wad gar him ken the odds between fou an' fare weel,' said the other matron. 'My troth! there's a haill squad o' men

in Laighbield wadna be so keen o' idleset,
gin they cam hame at e'en to get a toom
coggie glowerin' in the face o' them.'

At mention of Laighbield the Shetland
girls exchanged glances, and the elder of
them for the first time surveyed the speakers.
In so doing, she attracted Mr Choppin's
roving eye. Mr Choppin himself was now
gently oscillating on the edge of a wheelbarrow, and he took the young lady's notice
in such good part, that he responded with
a fixed smile, a nod which nearly over-
balanced him, and an invitation to come and
share his resting-place. To be hailed fami-
liarly by a working-man, and asked to sit
beside him in a wheelbarrow, was something
quite novel in the experience of Miss Ursula
Elvester. It required a little time to grasp
the reality of the thing ; and during that
time Mr Choppin, who really imagined he
was being very obliging and kind, took the
additional liberty of informing the young lady
that she was 'a desperate braw lass,' and
that he ' would like gran' to hear her sing.'

Thus far he ventured, but no farther: the
proud face turned upon him, with ineffable
surprise and expression, such as a goddess
might have worn if so she had been accosted
by the meanest of earth's sons, and had due
effect; Mr George Choppin was abased and
quenched. But now Miss Elvester reappeared and piloted her girls to a cab.
And so ended scene first of their experiences
in Netherlaw.

On and away they rattled; out of Royal
Square, with its rival hotels, its centre-piece
of ornamental gardening, its weather-beaten
statues of majesty and others; past the
parish church of St Barnabas, big and bald,
across one and another street, where din, like
that which once arose in the plain of Shinar,
smote the afflicted ear; and a great variety
of public buildings—new and old—florid as
a bridecake, or reornamented as a barn—
crowded upon the eye. When Miss Elvester
was at leisure to study the faces beside her,
she said to herself,—

'Ah, just so; I expected no less.'

For Ursula's expression told plainly that
life at this moment was very bitter, and tears
were glistening under Christian's lashes.

'Come, let us try to be a little cheerful if
we can,' said the eldest sister blithely.

'But how can we?' returned the younger,
faltering as she spoke. 'Things are so—so
—sad, Jenny.'

'And you want to make them sadder
still, by looking at them through tears?
No, Christian, that is not the way to face
trouble.'

'Have you no sensibility that you can
expect cheerfulness from us, placed as we
are?' said Ursula mournfully. 'Are you
made of stone?'

'Of the nether-millstone,' replied Miss
Elvester. 'Sensibility is an ornament I can't
afford to wear. Sense is enough for me
just now; the other I have locked away
against better times.'

'Perhaps it is as well,' murmured Ursula
gloomily, 'considering the people amongst
whom we are to live.'

'Some persons who spoke of Laighbield were just beside us on the platform,' explained Christian. 'One was a very impertinent man. Think of it, Jenny!—he asked Ursula to sit by him, and wished to hear her sing.'

'Oh, it is hard to bear!' groaned Ursula, alluding to her lot in general rather than to Mr George Choppin's politeness in particular. 'What have we ever done that we should be tried so?'

'That is a question of cause and effect, into the subtleties of which I can't enter,' said Miss Elvester. 'You must go to the Rev. Donald Berwick, I imagine, for light; problems of the kind lie more in his way than in mine.'

They were now out of the business part of the town, and driving up a narrow street of plain, three-storey houses, with enclosures before each, where grew grass and flowers, and shrubs baked rather brown, to make glad the heart of the dwellers and the passer-by.

'This is Chapel Street,' said Miss Elvester.
'How do you like it?'

Ursula having taken her sister's allusion
to the Rev. Donald Berwick seriously amiss,
said nothing. Christian therefore must speak.

'It is——' very pleasant, she would have
added, but could not, even to please Jenny,
tell an untruth; so after considerable search-
ing of heart, she substituted, 'not so bad.'

'Truly, my dear, it is not so bad as some
of the purlieus where poor tired Ulrica and
I went lodging hunting when we arrived,'
said Miss Elvester. 'Here is No. 50, then'
(for they had stopped before a close about
half-way along the street). 'We are reduced
to what some people might consider the
ignominy of a "flat." But never mind, the
disgrace will not be indelible. Now, go
upstairs at once. The driver will try to
overreach me—it is cab-driver nature—and I
won't be overreached, so a contest impends,
which I would spare your feelings.'

'Do you mean to wrangle with the man
about a paltry sixpence?—*you!*' and both

voice and features showed that Ursula felt she was now indeed sounding the deeper depths.

'I must do it,' replied Miss Elvester; 'such be the sweet uses of adversity. But away with you before we have our char- ioteer sarcastically inquiring, "What coin is this?"—three stairs up—right-hand door— name, Mrs Fairbairn.'

So instructed, the girls left their sister and the cabman to come to terms about the fare, and with languid steps commenced the toilsome ascent of the long, dimly- lighted, spiral staircase which led to Mrs Fairbairn's furnished apartments.

CHAPTER II.

URSULA'S MISTAKE.

'Proud abroad and proud at home,
  Proud wherever she chanced to come;
  When she was glad and when she was glum.'

THE entrance of Ursula and Christian Elvester roused a small
person who had been prone
upon the sofa of Mrs Fairbairn's tidy but
threadbare sitting-room. This sister, as
much younger than these two as their other
sister was older, received them with an air
of much and dignified importance. *She*
sleeping? No, and indeed, no! She had
but lain down to think, and having closed
her eyes—she could think more consecutively
with shut eyes—had forgotten to open them

again. As for daylight slumbering, that was
a thing— But Miss Elvester, victorious
from the battle of opinion with the cabman,
appeared, and cut Ulrica's explanation short.

As she attended to the wants of her travellers the manner of their eldest sister was
steadfastly cheerful ; and Christian, by the
time tea was over, had caught the infection
to the extent of being able to laugh now
and then. Ursula fared differently. Is life
worth living ? would have evoked from
her an unhesitating no. She ate mechanically what was set before her, but she
neither joined in the comparing of notes
which went on, nor yet took the slightest
interest in listening. Miss Elvester did
not approve of this brooding apart and
self-absorption, so after a while she remarked,—

' As I travelled through the wilderness of
this world, I lighted on a certain place where
was a den ? Isn't that how you feel about
it, Ursula ? '

' Well, I don't say you have come to a

bower of bliss exactly! I know that the wall-paper is unspeakable, and that the haircloth covered chairs and sofa are not just the kind of seats to be described as the lap of luxury; also, I agree with you that one's idea of young Lochinvar is not altogether realised in yon work of art, where the hero is represented at the moment when—

"So boldly he entered the Netherby Hall,
'Mong brides' men, and kinsmen, and brothers and all."

Still the room might have been worse. It *was* worse, before I suppressed a variety of lively-coloured wool-work, and sent a collection of wonderful artificial flowers to bloom unseen, instead of above the gay, tinsel-filled fireplace.'

'I am not complaining of the room,' said Ursula, with martyr-like meekness.

Ulrica, who, having been her father's spoilt favourite, took far too much upon her, hereupon observed,—

'You ought to be so very grateful that you have a house to come to. Jenny and I hadn't. While you were comfortable at Hily-ascord, we came to Netherlaw and sought out rooms for all of us. Such seeking! I never was so tired—never in all my life, tireder I know than you who are so cross.'

'And when you were tired, weren't you too ever so slightly cross?' urged Christian.

'I am not a grown-up person,' replied Ulrica. 'Jenny was never cross.'

'Jenny could not be cross, I think,' said Christian, admiringly. 'She would not know how.'

Miss Elvester affirmed that Jenny could very easily be cross, if she were only able to discover the advantage of it; and then she bade the girls go and sleep off their crossness and fatigue together. Christian contumaciously refused to obey. Ursula, on the other hand, seemed glad to seize the earliest opportunity of shutting her eyes on the world; so she followed Miss Elvester to a small, dull back room overlooking a dingy bleaching green, where two charwomen were beating carpets and an organ-grinder was drearily droning selections from *Norma* and *Masaniello.* The chamber was precisely like a prison-cell, thought Ursula—who had never seen a prison-cell ; and so thinking, she sat down by the shabby little bed in the corner, and, hiding her face on the coverlet, broke into passionate weeping.

Ulrica had come after her sisters unbidden ; and being so wise a woman in her own conceit, she undertook to bring silly Ursula to reason.

'Why should you cry?' she remonstrated. 'You make yourself too conspicuous.' (She did not quite convey her meaning here, but she loved long words, and so, like all who will be fine above measure, fell into confusion now and again.) 'I've not cried one single time since leaving Shetland, a whole week ago ; nor has Jenny ; and it is we who have had everything to do, and to think of.'

'*We* are strong persons,' said Miss Elvester ; 'and we must bear with our weaker brethren.'

'But no one ought to be weaker brethren,'

objected Ulrica. 'Isn't it foolish of them?'

'Go, get you gone, you small untimely moralist! Vanish!' cried Miss Elvester; and with good-humoured force the intruder was ejected and the door secured.

Miss Elvester had in a general way scant sympathy with anything lachrymose. She could, however, make allowances on occasion. For a time, therefore, she did not speak, but employed herself in unpacking Ursula's dressing-case. The sobs having at length ceased, she approached her afflicted sister, saying,—

'You will feel better now; a hearty cry is the cheapest medicine in the world—and the best sometimes, I am told.'

'Is there any need for ridiculing me because I am miserable?' returned Ursula coldly (for she was in the mood to see everything awry).

'My dear, I am not ridiculing you: on the contrary, I am extremely sorry for you. Indeed, Ursula, I would willingly make your path smoother and brighter if I could. But hear me : that things have gone badly enough with us, nobody will deny; you, however, take a too gloomy view—you think we have come to a pass than which there could not possibly be a worse.'

' I do not merely think it, I am sure enough of it. Everything—everything gone from us ; our home, our own Eastravoe, sold to strangers. Oh, it is too cruel ! '

' And if no other home had been in readiness—if, with the loss of our father's possession, all had been lost—how then ? '

' It would have been little worse than it is ; for I don't see how we shall be able to subsist on that pittance of yours ; and as for the house, is it not the merest hut in an odious country town ? '

Miss Elvester might have resented this contemptuous reference to the annuity and the morsel of property in Cornrigshire, her inheritance from her mother, which her father's daughters were henceforth to share with herself ; but she only smiled, and said,—

'I am full of the spirit of enterprise when I think of that hut. Glorious possibilities unfold themselves before my prophetic soul. Mark my words, Ursula; you shall one day beg my pardon for the scorn you now cast upon the Brae. I hope to bring the garden to grand perfection. Now, my garden, like Mr M'Dow's, has a great many " berry bushes in't " (but I forgot; you young people don't read Miss Ferrier); and as a certain clerical friend of yours is an authority on the subject of fruit trees, I must ask you to use your influence with him to—'

She was suddenly interrupted. Her sister rose up and stood before her, erect, flushed, and with flashing eyes. Cold, haughty Ursula could show fire enough, when put to it, one well saw.

'You are not to dare to jest to me about Mr Berwick,' she said in a low, repressed tone. 'Do you know what he has done? he has—asked me to marry him!'

Miss Elvester betrayed no surprise.

'At Hilyascord?' she inquired.

' No ; but before we left Eastravoe, just
after you were gone. But I have spoken
of it to no one, not even to Christian ;
and I only tell you, so that you may leave
off making reference to him. You had
better.'

' Am I to understand that you and he
have said good-bye ? '

' Would you have had anything else ? '

' I would have had you consult your own
feelings in the matter, as I trust you have
done.'

' I have done exactly as I would if my
father had been alive, and this desolation
had not fallen upon us — only he would
not have ventured to ask me then. Even
as it is, he ought not to have forgotten
the difference that there is between him
and me.'

' The difference ? Yes ; it is past meas-
urement. But did you remind the infatu-
ated man himself of this difference between
you ? '

' Excuse me, I have said all that I care

to say on the subject; so, if you please, don't ask questions; do just let the matter drop.'

'There needs no questioning indeed. I know as well as if I had been told how Mr Berwick entreated you to honour him (save the mark!), by giving him a husband's right to shield you from the poverty you so much dread. That fine fellow metaphorically—not literally, I hope—knelt at your feet; and you could not stoop to him.'

'I could not stoop to him.'

'I am sorry, Ursula, and sorrier for you than for Mr Berwick. My dear, you have made a mistake.'

'Is it a mistake to remember that, if nothing else remains to us, there is still our name? I am an Elvester, and though I have always liked and esteemed Mr Berwick, to marry him would be out of the question.'

'You fancy there would be degradation in an alliance with a farmer's son; but I don't quite see it somehow.'

'*You* would be content that we should marry, not farmers' sons, but farmers themselves, it seems to me!'

'Truly, if they were men such as Mr Berwick, I really don't know that I should mourn loudly over your declension; for, my dear Lady Lofty, I am apprehensive— I am very apprehensive—that if you ever do marry, it will not be to take your place amid the noble of the land.'

'You are to be envied, that you can make a jest—even of our misery,' said Ursula with a pitiful attempt at indifference.

'Yes; that is one of my pleasant little peculiarities. But do you not know that people must sometimes jest if they would not groan?'

What she had now heard had both vexed and disappointed Miss Elvester. She had the highest possible opinion of Mr Berwick; he and Ursula were exactly suited to each other; and, more than that, she very much inclined to the belief that Ursula herself felt the suitability—that the so-called liking and esteem—but what was the use of dwelling on the subject? The mistake had been committed, and no words of hers would undo it; so, bridling her tongue, she proceeded to needful action.

Unwinding a tangled skein is held the standing test of a woman's patience and temper; but some of us, who might come triumphantly through the ordeal of the skein, would break down utterly under the ordeal of ministering to an unthankful, unreasonable sister. Yet even here Miss Elvester did not fail; never was a woman more slow to wrath than she; indeed, it seemed as if, in spite of her own assertion to the contrary, she could not lose her temper, even if she tried.

CHAPTER III.

'A little, tiny, pretty, witty, charming darling she.'

URING the rest of that evening Miss Elvester was busy at her desk. Christian sat at the window counting the chimney-stalks—which, for this one holiday week, had ceased to waft their clouds of sooty incense to the skies—and much pitying the thousands of Netherlaw. Ulrica, lost in a volume of wonder-lore, was unconscious of outer things, and so continued till the voice of authority called her from fairyland and ordered her to dreamland instead. Christian saw her safely off, and then, the gas being lit, and the chimney-stalks no longer practicable, laid hands on a piece of knitting for lack of other resource.

> ' Had I the wings of a dove, I would fly
> ' Far, far away; far away.'

As Miss Elvester presently paused in her writing to hum—

> 'Where not a cloud ever darkens the sky,
> ' Far, far away ; far away.'

Christian looked up smiling, and caught her sister's eyes.

' Is that your own sentiment or mine ? ' she inquired.

' Yours, yours,' said Miss Elvester. ' There is a certain hardness of fibre about me—as I daresay you are aware—which renders me for ever incapable of such pretty sentiment as wishing to be a bird, or a daisy, or a butterfly born in a bower. My practical mind is exercised practically ; as, for in-stance, about that knitting of mine. What is amiss with it, Christian ? The pattern is at a crisis, and I am anxious about it, you see.'

'Ulrica's kitten has been making a football of it, I think. But I am putting it right again; and while I've been busy with it, I have forgotten to envy the dove her wings.'

'I daresay. Being busy is the best cure I know of for vain wishings,' and Miss Elvester resumed work.

The dropped stitches having been taken up, Christian sat still for a time, busy no longer, thoughtfully gazing at her sister. Poor Jenny! nobody ever heard a murmuring word from her lips; but there were lines on her brow, and dark circles about her eyes, and there was nothing left of her face's former softness of contour. Indeed, this scarcely looked like the Janet Elvester of a year ago, so terribly had the past month's anxiety told upon her. It became necessary, ere long, to find means of giving expression to the feelings which a contemplation of the change awakened; so Christian went quietly round to the back of her sister's chair, and began to trifle caressingly with the circlet of jet beads about the sitter's neck—with the fringe on her dress—with the plaits of her hair. The mute attentions were neither disallowed nor taken any notice of; and for a good many minutes Christian stood thus, watching the progress of the rapid, unresting pen. At last the work was done.

'Here is a pile of business off my conscience,' said Miss Elvester, the final letter having been addressed. 'It is rather a troublesome thing, this being an executrix; pray, Christian, that you may never be called upon to undertake the like. Why' (looking at her watch) 'I have even been longer than I thought; and you are not going to have any beauty-sleep, that is certain.'

'I am such a beautiful, beautiful creature that I need none,' said Christian, who, by the way, thought wonderfully little about her looks. 'And I wanted to wait for you, at anyrate; for, oh, Jenny, you can't fancy what a comfort it is to be with you again.'

'Do you feel it so? Then I have not lived in vain.'

'Of course you are laughing; you will

never let one have the satisfaction of paying you even the tiniest, most innocent of
compliments.'

'Certainly not.   Compliments don't suit
matter-of-fact elderly women.'

'Elderly, Jenny!   Why, you are—'

'Never mind the age, then; sensible, let
us say.'

Christian was kneeling before her sister
now, earnestly regarding the white, shapely
fingers by which her own pretty hands were
clasped.'

'Do I look like a person with something
on her mind?' she asked suddenly.

'I'm not certain how persons with something on the mind may be supposed to look,'
replied Miss Elvester, laughing.   'Not being versed in fiction, I don't know how a
heroine bears herself when she is mentally
distressed.'

'She has—let me consider—she has a
shadow on her fair young brow, her lake-
like eyes grow dim and hollow, her airy
tread becomes languid, and—and—'

'And does she keep her sister up through the early morning hours hearing her chatter?'

'She chatter! A heroine has a voice like flowing water, or silver bells—a " dulcet " voice, that is the word for it.'

' Delightful creature that she must be to have about one! But tell me now, what is this load of yours? Something very un-heroic, I venture to surmise.'

'As unheroic as myself, Jenny. One more question, please. What, upon your conscience, do you think I am fit for?'

'I don't know that you are fit for any-thing at all, my poor child.'

' Do you not believe me good for any-thing?'

'Oh, if you insist upon the whole truth, I do believe you are good enough for—I will show you what,' and Miss Elvester took the face of the querist between her hands, and laughingly kissed it once and again ; an unusual proceeding, for she was sparing of such demonstrations, reserving them for high days and holidays, as she herself would say. 'That is what you are good for,' she continued, 'to be petted and spoilt by people who are foolish enough to spoil and pet you.'

'It is so you always treat me, when I would make myself of use,' said Christian gravely. 'But I am now old enough to judge for myself, I think ; and this is what is on my mind. I—don't be astonished at me, Jenny—I intend—oh, it is nothing dreadful—to earn my own living.'

'You are a free and enlightened little person, to be sure !' exclaimed Miss Elvester, an expression of amusement, well mixed with satire, shining in her eyes. 'You intend to earn your own living, do you?   And since when have you been pleased to cherish this magnificent resolve, may one make bold to inquire ? '

Christian raised appealing eyes to the pale, sarcastic face which was bent towards her.

'Scold me if you must, but don't laugh at me,' she said.

'Your pardon !   I ask for information.

How long is it since you began to think of working for yourself?'

'Ever since rightly grasping all that our changed circumstances means, though I have never spoken of it till now.'

'No one, then — there are officious meddlers enough, I know—put the idea into your head?'

'No one. The idea is all my own. I mean to be a governess, Jenny.'

'I see; in order to escape the limitations of your present lot, you, like the sensible little girl you are, must find an entirely new sphere for yourself. But do you feel that you have a vocation for the position you aspire to?'

'I am fairly well educated, am I not?'

'Granted; but let me hazard the mild suggestion, that being fairly well educated oneself, and being even fairly well able to educate others, are things totally distinct. To imagine that, without a special training, or at any rate a special talent, you can be a successful teacher in the proper sense of the word, is as great a delusion as to fancy, like some men, that all required of him who would preach to his fellow-sinners, is un-bounded confidence, added to a pair of strong lungs. You may have chanced to hear such self-elected prophets; were they likely to advance the planet's evangelisation, think you?'

'But, indeed, the comparison is not a fair one. I am as humble as can be. I want to teach the alphabet; couldn't I do that?'

'Why, yes, you might. And so to teach the alphabet is the sum of your ambition?'

'Not quite. I'm presumptuous enough to hope that I might even dare a slightly higher flight. And if I be without either training or talent, I have one thing to re-commend me. I dearly love children.'

'No doubt. It happens to be an un-pleasant fact, however, that, while in theory children are dearly lovable, in practice they are sometimes exactly the reverse. I shouldn't care about any of my girls being a nursery governess, Christian, and I beg you to get rid of this crotchet of yours. For the present, at all events, content yourself with such a home as I can offer you.'

'I can't get rid of my—crotchet; it has taken too firm hold upon me. I must be independent.'

'Independent! So it is a question of woman's rights we have to deal with?'

'Yes, Jenny; of her right to work for herself.'

'Very well put, my witty one. And it seems so glorious a thing, this independence! quite worth paying any price for! But have you ever really counted the cost, Christian?'

'Again and again and again, Jenny.'

'So often? Well, it is hardly to be expected, I suppose, that, having set your heart on the assertion of your rights, you should let a half-sister's objections have any weight with you.'

'It is unkind to say so. My half-sister ought to know that she is more to me than any one in the world, and that there is no-

thing I will do, so long as she objects to
it.'

Miss Elvester's cheeks took the colour of
roses; so they always did when anything
touched the lady's heart.

'Do you not understand,' went on Christian, 'how it is just because I love you, that
I am anxious to leave you now. I can't
longer stand idly by, while you bear all the
burden. I can only be miserable while it is so.
Call my wish to work a crotchet, if you like ;
I shall not mind, if you will but humour it.'

This, and a great deal more than this,
Christian said for herself. Having thought
much about the matter beforehand she
argued her case well ; and when she had
done, her sister, who had listened with the
utmost patience, observed,—

'Perhaps, who knows, a taste of the
sweets of governesshood might send you
back to me, effectually cured of your passion for independence.'

'You consent to let me have my way?'
said Christian eagerly.

'Not so hasty. I consent to nothing yet. You have taken me by surprise, and I can't say either one thing or another. I must consider before I decide anything so important. I move, therefore, that the question be adjourned to a new day.'

Adjourned it was accordingly. In the meantime, Miss Elvester freed herself from her sister's girdling arms, and proceeded to put away her writing materials. Christian drew up the blind and looked forth. In Shetland it was tenderly light all through these summer nights. The sun merely dipped into the sea and was out again. But here twilight did not so melt into dawn. Netherlaw lay closely muffled in gloom—gloom that might be felt; and a painful sense of pent-upness oppressed the stranger, as her eyes wandered over the shadowy streets which stretched away—away —away in every direction. One could not breathe freely in this heavy atmosphere—this forest of chimney-stalks. Oh, for a waft of

the northern breezes!—or the familiar sea-
sound!—or,—

'By your good leave,' said Miss Elvester, turning out the gas.   It does not suit
me to burn the candle at both ends; and
as you are to share my room, it must not
suit you either.   Hie you to bed!'

CHAPTER IV.

ULRICA'S AMBITION.

Large streams from little fountains flow ;
Tall oaks from little acorns grow :
And though I now am small and young,
Of judgment weak and feeble tongue,
Yet all great learned men, like me,
Once learned to read their A B C.

'I FIND,' said Miss Elvester, after due consideration of the project which Christian's heart was set upon, 'that I dare not be the one to bar the way of an eager young soul afire with the spirit of independence. Do your will, then, and prosperity attend you.'

But Ursula!—pen cannot picture the dismay of Ursula when she heard of such a thing. Of course Christian tried, and tried again, to make her motives intelligible. It was useless; Ursula could, or would, see only that her sister meant to descend to the ranks of the paid labourers; that an Elvester of Eastravoe intended to work for hire. But Jenny would not surely consent to such dishonour. To her, therefore, Ursula appealed.

'Have we Elvesters ever yet lowered ourselves in the world's eyes?' she asked.

'I daresay we have, a thousand times— as you count lowering,' was the unpromising reply; 'you thought it a lowering of myself, when I disputed the fare with a cabman the other day.'

'You choose to misunderstand, but I am sure you know what I mean.'

'About the honour of our sires, is it? Why are you disquieted on that head? Have you a dream of trying to make atonement for the slips from honour of your ancestors?—because I wouldn't myself advise you to attempt anything so impossibly grand. Won't you rather be

satisfied with the humbler achievement of
keeping your own conduct as flawless as
may be?'

'I am not thinking either of myself or
my ancestors, but of Christian. You can
never intend to let her do what she is
talking of?'

'I intend to let her do as she pleases.'

This assurance seemed to stupify Ursula;
for fully a minute she did not utter a sound;
then, with tragic intonation, came the words,
'Evidently you don't care how low we sink
now!' and she turned to seek the solitude
of her dreary back room, there to brood
over this new root of bitterness.

Miss Elvester put down the Shetland
newspaper she had been scanning.

'You go just a little too far,' she said.
'I haven't the slightest intention that we
shall sink, so long as we can keep above
water. No, don't go. Come here, and let
me talk a little common sense to you.'

Ursula did not want to have common
sense talked to her. At this trying moment

she heartily disliked its very name. Still,
as she could not exactly refuse to listen,
she sat down ; but with a patience-on-a-
monument air about her, calculated to
excite ridicule or sympathy, as the be-
holder chanced to be in a satirical or a
sentimental mood.

'I suppose you remember the story of
Rosamond and the purple jar?' said Miss
Elvester.

Ursula supposed she did, but failed to
see its connection with the present question
at issue.

'Why, don't you observe I have given
way about this purple jar on which Christian's fancy is fixed ? I act as Rosamond's
mother acted—only up to a certain point,
however: I daresay I am wrong, but I
never could keep a mistaken one to her
bargain, after she had found it to be no
bargain at all, but a blunder. So Christian
shall try her luck ; and then, so soon as
she discovers that she has overrated her
own strength and courage, she shall be

welcome to return to us again. But if—
which may be the case—this scheme of
hers should prove to be more than a piece
of mere romance ; if she should be brave
enough to persevere in her work, and
should make it plain that she is in the
sphere Providence had meant her to fill,—
why, I will never bid her leave it.'

'What has happened to us already we
could not help,' observed Ursula bitterly ;
'now, we are voluntarily losing caste, and
descending from our position.'

'My dear, I am weary of this harping
on caste. Live nobly, Ursula, and never
mind the rest.'

'Is rank nothing, then ?' said Ursula,
still more bitterly than before.

'It is something, certainly ; but it is less
than the man. And in any case it has
never been proved, so far as I know, that
a gentlewoman cannot work for wages and
be a gentlewoman still. Show me wherein
the degradation of receiving payment for
honest work consists.'

But there was no response. Miss Elvester's common sense had fallen on ears that would not receive it. She could not bring her ideas to the level of her lot,—this proud, foolish Ursula. It appeared to her that things had gone wrong beyond power of mortal to better them ; and now they might take their own course; she for her part was done with protesting.

Since their father's death Ursula had taken the place of governess to Ulrica (it was only the post of a paid governess that she objected to), giving herself great trouble for small thanks ; or rather, for quite the reverse of thanks, since Ulrica was heard frequently to complain that the yoke of her instructress was heavier than girl could bear.

'Ursula thinks of nothing—nothing— nothing,—but how to keep me writing tiresome exercises and learning strange French conjugations,' grumbled the rebel. 'I almost believe she invents irregular verbs as she goes along.'

'That is very clever of her,' replied Christian, to whom this appeal for sympathy was addressed.

Ulrica considered the remark flippant, and passed it by.

'There is no piano here,' she resumed, 'but oh! there will be practising and practising when we get to Laighbield. I wish Jenny would attend to my education then!'

'I wouldn't wish that if I were you,' said Christian; 'Jenny would say far more than Ursula ever says, if lessons were unprepared.'

'But I shouldn't so much mind that. Ursula doesn't *say*, she only *looks;* and I am sensitive. I don't like being looked at by her solemn eyes, as if I were making her very unhappy, and she were wondering at me.'

The feeling was perfectly understood by Christian; she too knew what it was to endure the speechless reproach of solemn-eyed Ursula.

'Ursula concerns herself with more than my education,' said Ulrica, passing to an-

other source of discontent. 'She won't let
me read any books but fairy-tales, and child-
ish stories about good prim little girls with
such lecturing mammas. And you get so
tired of these at last.'

'Tired of Hans Andersen? Then I'm
sorry for you. But patience, Ulrica; you'll
come to the other kinds in time.'

'Oh, it is all very well for you to say
"patience;" but suppose you found in the
cupboard of your room a delightful tale
called *The Bravo's Bride; or, Doomed by
Destiny*, and suppose you had got to the
middle of the third chapter, when Ursula
came upon you, and chose to say that you
mustn't read "that trash," and when you
wouldn't give it up, called Jenny, who then
came and took it away; how should you
like that?'

'Poor little victim!' laughed Christian,
patting the child's cheek. 'What a very
bad time she has with her hard-hearted
sisters.'

'I don't think people should call a book

"that trash," till they can write a better themselves,' continued Ulrica, giving her flowing fair hair an indignant shake. 'And Ursula can't write at all; not anything original, I mean, only exercises and rules of grammar, and Latin roots (I'm sure I can't guess why the Latins should have been so fond of roots). But let me tell you, Christian, *I* am going to do something for the honour of our family. I have determined I will be an authoress.'

'That will be delightful,' said Christian; but she was not much impressed apparently.

'When I told our old Jeromina at home, she took much more interest than you do,' said Ulrica, in an injured tone.

'It is so far off, you see,' apologised Christian.

'Not so far off as you may fancy. I grow up rapidly, and I have already multitudes of ideas in my mind. But, Christian, one thing puzzles me. Jeromina says grown-up stories were always about love; I was sorry to hear that, because I don't know anything about love.'

'Nor do I.   But suppose, just for a change, you were to write a story, a grown-up story, without love.'

'I did speak of that to Jeromina, but she didn't think it would do; it would be "affa dry," she said.   If I could have gone on with *The Bravo's Bride*, I should have learnt something, don't you think?   Oh, Jenny' (for Miss Elvester had that moment entered), 'have you overheard our conversation?'

'A few words of it only,' was the reply. '*The Bravo's Bride* forsooth.   The grammar and the dictionary would better suit you.'

'Think, Jenny; our youngest is going to be an authoress,' said Christian.

Miss Elvester raised her eyebrows.

'Have I under my charge a woman of intellect in embryo?' she exclaimed.   'The sense of responsibility appals me, I confess. But, my little girl, may I ask you kindly to

suppress your talent for the time, and to put
your room to rights. Books and papers are
in dire confusion yonder; and if you are a
genius, that is no reason why you should be
untidy in your habits.'

The future authoress rose to obey. In
passing, she stopped and put her arms about
the mentor's waist.

'I'll be as tidy as ever you like,' she
whispered, 'if you will only let me have
back *The Bravo's Bride.*'

'Let you have back what?' cried her
sister.

'*The Bravo's Bride,*' she said coaxingly;
'please, *please*, Jenny, give it to me back.'

Her wiles were wasted.

'*The Bravo's Bride* is out of the question,'
replied Miss Elvester; 'you shall have
Little Goody Two-Shoes, rather.'

'Papa would not have been so hard to
me,' murmured Ulrica, and her lips quivered
and her arms were withdrawn. 'He would
not be pleased if he were to know. He
would wish you to be less unkind to me.'

The colour sprang into the guardian's face. But Miss Elvester did not generally speak before thinking. She held her peace for a moment, therefore, considering whether she should condescend to justify her conduct. Then she sat down and drew Ulrica back to her side, saying kindly but with authority,—

'I hope I shall not hear anything of this sort again ; and I believe I shall not, when I have once shown you how mistaken you are. Our father would certainly approve of what you call my hardness to you. Let me try to make you understand.'

But what she said need not be repeated here ; it suffices that she did not let the hungerer for forbidden fruit depart, till she had brought her round to reason and submissiveness.

CHAPTER V.

A PAIR OF NETHERLAW NOTABILITIES.

He that has ill-luck gets ill-usage.

IT occasionally happens in this strange world, that the public passes with regardless eye some picture by some young artist who fondly fancies himself a greater than Turner; that it will not read the book whose author felt certain he had written a thing which would take its breath away with wrapt delight; that it is perversely determined to have no cognisance of the 'eager young soul, afire with the spirit of independence.'

So Christian, who had in her ignorance imagined that one needed but to cry, 'I

have an ambition to teach ; bring me your
children, pray you,' and the children would
be brought, soon became painfully aware
that it was not at all thus, but that in the
commodity of governesses, the supply was
greatly in excess of the demand.

She advertised ; she replied to advertisements ; she made application at various
scholastic agencies, but nothing came of it
—nobody answered her.   She was almost
in despair, when one auspicious morning,
glancing down the column in the *Reflector*
that she always turned to first, her eyes
were arrested by the cheering lines,—

'Governess wanted for a gentleman's family
in the West End ; must be thoroughly quali-
fied to instruct in elementary English, and
to ground in the rudiments of French, Latin,
German, Music (vocal and instrumental) and
Drawing.   Good accent indispensable.   Un-
exceptional references required.   Apply per-
sonally, between the hours of twelve and
three, at Miss Colquhoun's Register Office,
Lockerbie Street.'

Hope at last! in a personal application assuredly there was hope; and she could eat no breakfast in view of it; though Miss Elvester warned her that she would never attain to a green old age if she allowed every stray contingency so greatly to excite her. Not much matter, Christian thought; she was not troubled about anything so remote as a green old age; her immediate concern was about her accent. References the most unexceptionable were not wanting; but her accent? Miss Elvester dared to say it would pass muster; Ursula said not a word; but you may be sure her good wishes did not attend her sister to Miss Colquhoun's Register Office.

Lockerbie Street was the promenade upon which fashionable Netherlaw daily aired itself; but as Miss Elvester's girls had hitherto walked abroad but little, and in Lockerbie Street not at all, Christian wended her way now for the first time through that gay thoroughfare. Preoccupied as she was, however, passing her qualifications in review,

speculating as to the children whose governess was to 'ground' them in so many
rudiments, and hoping that Christian Elvester
might be the person selected to do the
grounding required, it seemed to her that
she had hardly quitted Mrs Fairbairn's
apartments before she arrived at the register office.

Here she paused to summon up courage,
because—there was no concealing it from
herself, now that the much prayed-for moment was come, it found her unmistakably
frightened. But the longer she lingered
outside the more afraid she grew, and when
at length she did cross the threshold, it was
with the feeling strong upon her, that she
was making a very desperate venture indeed.

Within was a good-natured looking, middle-
aged person, who immediately turned from
the huge ledger in which she was writing
entries, to inform Christian that the adver-
tiser for a governess, Mrs Baillie Geddes,
waited in the back room to give audience
to candidates, and that one such was at

present under examination. Even as it was
being told, there issued from the regions
behind a smartly dressed, rather pertly
mannered girl.

' I've met a good many patterns of horrid
pretension since coming to your town, Miss
Colquhoun,' she said, ' but that woman beats
them all. Guess what her first words were?'

Miss Colquhoun declined the riddle.

' Then I must tell you. I had the pre-
sumption to sit down, and her ladyship
desired me to " stand, please," and the rest
of her was to match. It was rather too
much of a good thing. Stand, indeed! Did
she take me for a housemaid, I wonder?'

Having thus delivered herself, this indignant young person snatched at the parasol
which had been awaiting her in a corner,
tossed to Miss Colquhoun a by no means
amiable adieu, and swept from the register
office.

Such a prelude could not be called re-
assuring, and it was with increased nervous-
ness that Christian passed into the audience

chamber where Mrs Baillie Geddes sate, queenlike, to receive her. Then broke upon her a confused consciousness of tawny surging silk, and crest of white ostrich plumes, and hard black eyes, and awe-inspiring nose; then a supercilious nod was vouchsafed her, and then Mrs Baillie Geddes entered upon the process of 'eyeing her over,' an operation which, to give the lady due credit, she performed in a style worthy of Mr Simon Tapertit himself. The result of the survey was not altogether satisfactory.

'H'm—ha—' said Mrs Baillie Geddes, elevating her aquiline nose and outstanding chin. 'You look very young—too young for me. Your age, if you please?'

'I shall be twenty in December,' answered Christian, wishing that she could have said thirty instead. And she was still more ashamed of her youth when Mrs Baillie Geddes rejoined,—

'As I thought. Too young. Absurdly so for a governess. But what experience have you had?'

Alas! for Christian, she had to confess to no experience at all.

'No experience!' echoed Mrs Baillie Geddes, and her hooked nose seemed to become more hooked than ever. 'Why, then, do you answer advertisements?'

'One must make a beginning,' ventured Christian, in excuse.

'The beginning ought to be made as an articled pupil,' returned Mrs Baillie Geddes with, if that were possible, an increase of sternness. 'What I require is a person who thoroughly understands her business, Miss Axminster' (Christian had on entering given her name with perfect distinctness, and Mrs Baillie Geddes was not hard of hearing), 'and who has method. My present governess has no method; and besides that, she is in failing health. A person in poor health has no right to offer herself as a governess; to do so is, I maintain, a species of fraud which ought to be punishable by law. Are you perfectly sound, Miss Exeter?'

Though much struck by this view of ill-health in a governess, Christian veiled her surprise, and answered that her physical condition was all that could be desired.

'H'm! You do not seem to me to have much stamina,' said Mrs Baillie Geddes. 'In my family a person with stamina is required—with *stamina*,' and, pausing, she pierced Christian through with those relentless eyes, as if in quest of hidden signs of stamina.

'How many pupils should I have?' inquired Christian, when she had, with some difficulty, screwed up her courage to the point of asking the question.

Mrs Baillie Geddes did not approve of the liberty, and she stared, as much as to say, 'What are things coming to?'

'The governess has nothing whatever to do with the elder Misses Baillie Geddes,' she replied majestically, 'but only with Masters Ferdinand and Leopold James, and Miss Millicent Louise. And now, pray, what references can you produce? That is a point upon which I am most particular

—references. I must have first-class re-ferences.'

Particular as she was, Christian could satisfy her here; so fully, indeed, that it seemed as if inexperience, and deficiency in stamina even, might be got over. Mrs Baillie Geddes did not commit herself, of course—that would have been rash; but, having sifted the educational qualifications of the present aspirant, she rehearsed at long length the duties which would devolve upon the person selected to discharge the office of governess to the younger mem-bers of the Baillie Geddes household, and mentioned, by the way, that as for emolu-ment, provided the person were thoroughly suitable, that would be on a liberal scale—a handsome and a liberal scale.

'But you are only one in a crowd,' she wound up, 'so I can come to no conclusion to-day, Miss—Westminster—Isbister—what do you say your name is?'

'Elvester,' replied Christian, trying to pronounce even more distinctly than before.

'Ha—well, as I say, I can settle nothing
to-day.   You, on the whole, have pleased
me best so far.   I am pleased with your
references.   You may call to-morrow forenoon, at Mr Baillie Geddes's place of business, Seven, Alexander Buildings, and you
will be informed whether I have decided to
engage you.   Seven, Alexander Buildings,
Miss Elster, about twelve o'clock.'

And a second nod, no less supercilious
than the first, gave Christian to understand
that for the present, at all events, Mrs
Baillie Geddes had done with her.

Miss Colquhoun was now parleying with
a domestic in search of a 'place,' and four
disengaged governesses were exercising their
patience till Mrs Baillie Geddes should find
it convenient to inspect them.   Christian
would have left the office without speaking,
but when she bowed, Miss Colquhoun came
to open the door for her.

'There is a chance of your not getting
this situation,' said the proprietress of the
register office, with a little shake of the head,

' so, in case of that, here' (presenting a slip
of paper) ' is the address of another lady
who is looking out for a governess.'

' You are very good,' murmured Christian,
with a rather forced smile.

' Not in the least,' said Miss Colquhoun
briskly. ' All in the way of business, Miss
Elvester; if I get you a situation you owe
me half-a-crown. I hope you will soon be
suited. Good-day.'

There was no doubt about it ; the prospect
of coming under the jurisdiction of such a
stickler for stamina as Mrs Baillie Geddes,
was the reverse of exhilarating. But
Christian dared not flinch already and draw
back. That would be disgraceful indeed !
So all the way to Chapel Street she kept
telling herself that it was very wrong to
judge from first impressions, and trying to
get up the persuasion that, Medusa stare and
magisterial manner notwithstanding, Mrs
Baillie Geddes might really possess even
more than the ordinary modicum of human
kindness.

Full of this charity, she slurred details, when questioned in family committee as to how she had fared; whereupon Ulrica, athirst for particulars (probably she was thinking of material for volumes which were to delight a future public), became very pointed in her remarks about people who would only draw their sketches in outline. What was the good of living in this world at all if one were to be so absolutely unobservant of the niceties of colour and shading in the characters whom one encountered?

Next forenoon, as Christian was making ready for Alexander Buildings, Miss Elvester gave notice of an intention on her part to play propriety on the occasion; she did not approve, she said, of girls running about unattended among the offices of business men. A protecting presence would not come amiss, Christian admitted; but, on the other hand, who would engage a governess who needed a sister to see her safely through the streets? The sister was willing to be invisible, if required, and expressed herself ready to remain outside during the interview with Mr Baillie Geddes; and under this condition her guardianship was gladly enough accepted.

Alexander Buildings was a dingy quadrangle in the centre of the town, so entirely uninteresting, that this pen, even if it delighted in descriptive passages much more exceedingly than it does, would not be tempted to portray it.

'Do you still wish single handed to confront your fate?' inquired Miss Elvester at the entrance to No. 7.

'I must learn to rely upon myself now, must I not?' said Christian; 'and Mrs Baillie Geddes will only engage a governess who has " stamina."'

'Go, then, and may all that is good go with you. Amen.'

Thus blessed, Christian took her way upstairs. On the first landing were several doors. One swung apart, and let out a message boy, who opened his eyes wide on the young lady, and then skipped away down, three steps at a time. On the white panels

of another was inscribed the address:
'Baillie Geddes & Co., Stockbrokers and
Commission Agents.'

'This looks worse even than the register
office,' thought Christian, but she would not
give herself time to hesitate, so went forward
at once and knocked. It was a timid little
tap, and it got no notice taken of it. She
knocked again, and more boldly this time.

'Push it open,' cried a voice within.

She pushed it open accordingly, and entering, found herself in the presence of she could
not tell how many clerks, who simultaneously
raised their heads, and with one accord stayed
their pens to take note of her. She turned
to the youth who was nearest, and gave him
her card to hand to his principal. He looked
at it on both sides, then conveyed it to a room
in the distance, marked 'Private,' and there
delivered it. During the following few
minutes a good deal of whispering and suppressed laughter went on. The funning
had nothing to do with Christian; but as she
could not know that it had not, it made her

uncomfortable enough. After what seemed
an hour (fancy had magnified seconds into
minutes) there issued from the private room
a tall, stout, flowing whiskered gentleman,
wearing a small fortune in shape of a
diamond ring on one of his short fat hands.
Dead silence fell; there was instant hurrying
on of every pen; the visitor concluded that
she now beheld Mr Baillie Geddes. Mr
Baillie Geddes indeed it was; and, without
wasting ceremony on Christian; in fact
scarcely taking the trouble of looking at her,
he lifted up his voice aloud, and proclaimed,—

'She said I was for to inform you that
she has engaged one that she saw before
that she went to the registry.'

And, his whole duty done, the flowing
whiskered gentleman retired into privacy
again.

CHAPTER VI.

A FRIEND IN NEED.

' If ye hae friends enow,
Though real friends, I believe, are few,
I'se no insist,
But gif ye want a friend that's true,
I'm on your list.'

IT had been very dreadful altogether.
Christian would never want to see
the obnoxious quadrangle, called
Alexander Buildings, again. Yet, determined to let nothing daunt her, she, that
very afternoon, set out to try her luck with
Mrs Smellie, Elysium Villa, Glovelands,
whose address she had got from Miss
Colquhoun of the register office. Here,
also, failure awaited her. A governess had

been fixed upon, Mrs Smellie told her, only an hour before.

This Mrs Smellie, a jolly, kindly soul, was much 'taken,' so she phrased it, with the pretty Shetland girl, and Christian found herself obliged, whether she would or not, to rest and have refreshments in a drawing-room so gaudy, so parti-coloured, as to set her thinking of a kaleidoscope, and so full of ornamental incongruities of every description, that one felt all - overish only to look at it.

A day or two after this, another advertisement appeared in the *Reflector.* A young lady was wanted as governess to three little girls. She must have no objections to travel, but that was the only must in the matter ; and applicants were invited to present themselves at No. 5 Chapel Street.

Without loss of time, Christian repaired to No. 5. It was a main - door flat, and a card, upon which was written in flourishing letters, and with an extra p, the word 'Appartments,' decorated one of the windows. A small servant-maid, in the last stage of slatternliness, opened the door and consigned the ladies—for Miss Elvester once more accompanied her sister, and there was no talk this time of her remaining out-side—to the nearest 'appartment,' a dark, unwholesome room, redolent of the fumes of vile cigars. Scattered about the floor lay a pack or two of very dirty cards ; on the table were refreshments for body and mind ; plenty of soda water and brandy, and a copy of that most edifying publication, *The Police News.*

'We must have come to the wrong place,' concluded Miss Elvester, as she observed these various details. 'The retainer seemed too stupid to understand a word I said to her ; but our business can't certainly be with any one here,' and she took hold of the bell-pull to recall the smutty little maid, but, as might have been anticipated, the wire was broken.

Just then was heard a shuffling sound

without, and next moment there slid forward into sight a dishevelled young man,
in a stained and tattered dressing-gown,
and with feet more out of than in a pair
of what had been slippers once, but could
hardly, even by courtesy, be called slippers
now.

'Your most obedient,' said this figure,
laying hand on heart, and executing an
exaggerated salaam.

'There is some mistake, I believe,' said
Miss Elvester.

'Oh, it's all serene,' returned the grimy
one; 'you call in reference to advertisement in to-day's *Reflector*. Pray, do be
seated, ladies. There's a pair of boots in
the easy-chair, miss, but you can pitch 'em
down, and welcome.'

But perhaps Christian, to whom this
liberty was accorded, thought it would be
a pity to displease the boots; at all events,
she continued standing.

'What will fit the party to appear for,'
the young man, still addressing himself to

Christian, 'is the girl who'll undertake to
do the teacher and friend and helpful companion all in one.   But you ain't very
particular now; are you, miss?   For there
is a many parts we visit where we haven't
any more accommodation than only just
the travelling van.'

Christian again left her sister to speak
for her; and,—

' I beg your pardon?' said Miss Elvester
inquiringly.

' The caravan, don't you know,' explained
he of the dressing-gown.   'Sister and self,
ladies, are joint-proprietors of a travelling
menagerie — widowed   sister, ladies, with
three small children.'

' The situation will not suit this young
lady,' said Miss Elvester, with a manner
well calculated to check further jauntiness.
' When next you advertise, you will perhaps be good enough to mention the cir-
cumstance of the caravan; considerable
waste of time—both your own and others'
—will so be prevented.   Good morning.'

And thus, with a suddenness which the travelling showman, judging from his looks, had been by no means prepared for, the conference came to an end.

Anew disappointed, Christian repeated the experiment of advertising in *The Reflector*. And she actually got an answer, too—but then *such* an answer!—an execrably written note, in which 'a pearsonal interview' was 'kindly requisted;' this pleasure, it need scarcely be said, her weakness in favour of authorised forms of orthography led her cruelly to decline.

What next? she wondered. But it seemed as if there was to be no next; nobody in all wide Netherlaw needed her services; no Samaritan appeared to supply her with the means of self-support. The house at Laighbield, tenantless since Whitsunday term, and now under repair, would be ready for occupancy in October; and September was nearly run, and hope almost gone out, when one forenoon a shiny-faced visitor, elaborately trimmed and lavishly bejewelled, made her appearance in Mrs Fairbairn's threadbare little parlour.

'I never was invited,' said Mrs Smillie, grasping with painful heartiness the hand held out to welcome her; 'but I've come, you see—I've come!'

Christian acknowledged the kindness, and introduced the stranger. Miss Elvester chanced to have gone out, which was unfortunate, as she would at least have been courteous. But so would not Ursula. *She* encourage the familiarities of that absurdly over-dressed person! If Christian must cultivate such a sort of friends, she need not also look for her family to share in the intercourse; so not a hair's-breadth would Ursula move beyond the most distant civility.

But Ulrica, ready to be affable, stepped forward, and, after Christian, submitted her hand to the visitor's pleasure.

A kitten was perched on the child's shoulder as Mrs Smillie said,—

'Would you not like a little doggie better?'

'I haven't any dogs—not *now*,' replied Ulrica. 'But this is not a common-place kitten—he is my own ; our landlady has given him to me, and I am training him ; his name is Slyboots.'

'What a droll name for a beast.'

'I wanted it to be droll. I wouldn't have him called Spotty, or Flossy, or Jetty —any of those stupid things people call their pets. Very well, Ursula' (as she caught a glance from across the room), 'I won't say any more, if you think I ought not.'

Then she withdrew to a corner, and confided to Slyboots her belief that Ursula would want a suite of apartments all to herself when she should get to heaven, so as to be quite select.

It was not mere idle curiosity that had brought Mrs Smillie to Chapel Street. It was that she had heard from one Mr Fyfe Armstrong, a young artist to whom she and 'Pa' were sitting for full-length portraits, of an opening which might suit Christian. Indeed, from all accounts, the situation would be 'exactly the thing,' she thought.

Christian thought so too, when she had heard details ; but she could not feel sanguine. She had been disappointed so often that it appeared to her almost impossible she should ever succeed.

'They want an Englishwoman,' said Mrs Smillie, suddenly recollecting that fact. 'But what about it ?' she added reassuringly. 'You speak as nice as any English lady, though you're Scotch.'

'Oh, we are not Scotch, indeed,' cried Ulrica, who disdained the connection. 'We are Shetlanders.' She had forgotten her promise to keep silent under the provocation of being called Scotch.

'Just that,' acquiesced Mrs Smillie, in the ready, careless way one agrees with the very young or the very old.

Again the small maiden's sense of dignity was wounded, and in spite of Christian's very evident disapproval, she was about to assert her nationality ; had got so far as—

'We are descended from the Scandinavian sea-kings, we Elvesters,' when her eldest sister came in, and she was once more suppressed.

Nothing beyond an interchange of civilities passed between Miss Elvester and Christian's new friend, for it was nearly two now, and Mrs Smillie had promised to lunch with 'Pa' at Price and Platterfill's exactly at two o'clock.

'And the gentlemen never like to be kept waiting,' she said, 'especially when there's a knife and fork in the question.'

The door having closed upon the visitor, Miss Elvester observed,—

'An unlooked-for pleasure ; though you don't seem to have found it a pleasure, Ursula. You don't appreciate the attention?'

'Am I likely to appreciate the attention of that dreadful woman?' cried Ursula the disdainful, tossing up her chin.

'Don't be vexed about her having called,' said Christian, 'for indeed it was good of her. I am really obliged. Don't you think I have reason to be ?'

' I can't quite acknowledge that the Elvesters of Eastravoe stand in need of the good
offices of any Netherlaw shopkeeper's wife,'
returned Ursula loftily.

' If we were the Elvesters of Eastravoe,'
Christian put her in mind ; ' but we are the
Elvesters of nowhere now.'

' We are the Elvesters of the Brae, Laighbield, Cornrigshire, now,' amended Ulrica ;
' aren't we, Jenny ? '

' We are the Elvesters who will only get
ourselves laughed at, if we go about pro-
claiming our descent from the Scandinavian
sea-kings,' was the reply.

' I wish you wouldn't always snub me,'
murmured Ulrica ; ' it spoils my disposition.'

' I like the kind Mrs Smillie,' said Christian,
returning to the defence. ' What does it so
greatly matter that she isn't dressed to please
you, Ursula, and that her manner isn't exactly what you've been accustomed to ?
Have you only one standard to judge by ?
Do dress and manner count for everything
with you ? '

'Social distinctions count for something with me too.'

'Well, I suppose birth is something to glory in ; but, for all that, I don't know what good ours is to us now, or will ever be.'

'Jenny! O Jenny! can you patiently listen to her?' ejaculated the sorely-scandalised Ursula.

'That can I,' said Miss Elvester calmly; 'for if I should fret my soul about every foolish speech I hear of from the triad, life's burden would be too heavy for me. Not that I consider Christian in the wrong just now, but you rather. I wish you could rid yourself of that fear of losing caste, my dear. Have you no independence of character? Can you not be content to " do weel, and let them say ? " '

There was no answer, but a moment or two afterwards Ursula left the room.

Christian then told Miss Elvester about the newly-arisen hope.

'And don't you think I should suit as exactly as if I had been made for the purpose ?' she asked, all having been described.

'Let me see if I have mastered the summary,' said Miss Elvester. 'Mrs Cassillis, of 11 Argyll Gardens (uncle's widow, of Cassillis of Laighbield), orphan, grandson; liberal salary; duties light. That is all, isn't it ?'

'Englishwoman preferred,' appended Christian dolefully. 'Why am I not an Englishwoman, Jenny ?'

'I have not time now to seek a key to that dark providence,' said Miss Elvester; 'for I have a piece of business that will take me out again immediately. By the way, there are some letters here which I must have copies of. Will you do the work for me while I'm gone ?'

'Of course I will do it ;—but while you're gone ? Would not evening serve ?'

'The letters must be posted before evening,' Miss Elvester replied.

Christian said not another word, though it was by no means with a willing heart that, relinquishing her purpose of an immediate visit to Argyll Gardens, she prepared to devote the afternoon to the copying of business letters. But she sought refuge in fatalism, consoling herself with the reflection that, what must be, must be ; and thus philosophically minded, carried the appointed task to her own room, and worked steadily on, till the door opened, and the question,—

' Well, my little copying machine, how prosper you ? ' announced that her sister was returned.

' I *never* prosper,' she answered, rather wearily. ' Look here, though, I have nearly got to an end.'

' Good girl ! ' said Miss Elvester, with approval, and she came and glanced rapidly over what had been written. ' Do you think now,' she inquired when all was done,—' do you privately think that I have caused you to lose a glorious opportunity of achieving independence ? '

' If you have, how shall I ever forgive you ? ' replied Christian, looking up smilingly

into her questioner's face.   She could not be
angry with Jenny—not although she tried.

'I have been to Argyll Gardens,' said
Miss Elvester.

'You have been—'

'To Argyll Gardens.   Did I not speak it
distinctly enough ?'

All eagerness, Christian sprang up and
exclaimed,—

'How very good of you !   And have I
any hope ?   Will Mrs Cassillis take me, do
you think ?'

'Miss Christian Elvester, you will find it
expedient to put a little starch of propriety
into your deportment : repose of manner is
desirable in a governess.'

'Jenny, tell me—tell me first ; and put my
deportment to rights afterwards.'

Then Jenny told her : 'Mrs Cassillis, a
lady in whose hands one would not fear to
leave one's sister—since leave her one must
at all—wished Christian to call at 11 Argyll
Gardens early on the following day.'

CHAPTER VII.

A GRACIOUS WOMAN.

'Madam!' (quod I) 'with all mine whole servise
I thank you now in my most humble wise.'

THE houses in Argyll Gardens were
large and handsome. The 'gardens' were so fresh of hue—thanks
to the perpetual care bestowed upon them—
that only a critic predetermined to find fault,
could describe them as smoked or sunburnt;
in short, there was nothing here distinctly
characteristic of Netherlaw.

A carriage and pair waited at the door of
No. 11, and it was a man-servant who con-
ducted Christian through the lofty, marble-
pillared hall, up the stained-glass lighted
staircase, to the spacious front drawing-room.

Not an Elysium villa drawing-room this. You had not to pick your steps gingerly, and gather in your skirts with care, lest you should displace or overthrow some wonderful and useless piece of crockery or upholstery. You had room here, and liberty. There was no glare, no glitter. The tints were rich, soft, harmonious; ornaments did not run riot, yet there was no deficiency of things graceful and pretty, curious and quaint. There were valuable pictures too; and for the rest, as many lovely flowers and ferns as heart could wish.

Near the door stood Mrs Cassillis, a stately woman robed in black. Her widow's head-dress became her like a crown. There was a grand air of repose about her, and she turned a pair of such serene brown eyes upon Christian, while, with gracious bow and smile, she begged to be excused for just one minute. Her plea was beside her, in female form — a very beautiful brunette, habited according to the latest Parisian fantasy.

'How exceedingly tiresome of cousin Glen,' this young lady was saying. '*Isn't* he provoking, Aunt Marjorie?'

'But you must recollect,' answered Mrs Cassillis, 'that an officer has not affairs so entirely at his own ordering that he can take leave of absence at any time he chooses, even if it should be to attend a cousin's birthday party.'

'Why, then, if he can't, he might as well be a common soldier at once, and stand in a sentry-box,' cried the beauty, tossing her head.

Christian could not but wonder what sort of girl this was—a wonder to be satisfied to the very utmost by-and-by. As yet, however, the fair creature remained a mystery; for immediately after her remark about the sentry-box, she airily threw a flying kiss to her kinswoman and departed, leaving Mrs Cassillis and 'that musty little governess' (so the beautiful brunette thought of Christian) to get to business.

Mrs Cassillis heard the history of the

Elvester family, and she more than doubted
that a daughter of the house of Eastravoe
would not soon feel at home in the position
of a governess.

'Before you charge yourself with the care
of my little grandson,' she said to Christian,
by way of friendly caution, 'you must allow
me to make quite clear to you what it is you
would undertake. The child is delicate and
must not have his energies in any way taxed.
Indeed, I want a governess less for educational purposes as yet, than because it appears
to me advisable that the boy should have
some one about him, younger than his grandmother and different from his nurse. You
see what I offer. Do you think you could
patiently devote hours every day to the
amusement and instruction, by the way, of
a child who is not only far from strong, but
—yes, I must confess it, sadly spoilt as well?'

Looking at the lady who was this spoilt
child's grandmother, Christian felt quite
hopeful that she could, and she said so.

'But would you not—I speak very frankly,

you see—find it terribly irksome to be confined for the most part to the company of an
old woman and a little boy? You are a
young creature; you have been accustomed
to be waited on all your life. Could you,
with anything like cheerfulness, endure such
an existence as I have pictured?'

'I should like to have leave to try,' was
the response ; and a pair of very alluring blue
eyes eloquently seconded the appeal of the
pretty pleading lips.

So after a little more talk the thing was
settled, and a week later, her sisters having
left Netherlaw for Laighbield, Christian entered upon her duties at Argyll Gardens.

CHAPTER VIII.

MR MUNGO MAUCHLINE.

' Your critic folk may cock their nose,
   And say, " How can you e'er propose,
You, wha' ken hardly verse frae prose,
                 To mak' a sang ?"
But, by your leaves, my learned foes,
                 Ye're may be wrang.'

FURNITURE and luggage had been
sent on before, under charge of a
highly-recommended general servant, named Mysie ; and now Miss Elvester
and her two remaining girls took their places
in the Cornrigshire train, Ulrica carrying
Slyboots in a basket.

From Netherlaw to Braidmoss by rail ;
from Braidmoss to Laighbield by stage-

coach ; such was the mode of the journey. At its appointed hour the train crossed that treacle-like current, styled by Netherlaw platform orators ' Our noble river,' pursued its course high among the chimney-pots, gave passengers a grand chance of refreshing themselves with a view of the slums, entered a mile-long tunnel, and at last emerged in the open country.

The country, indeed ; but even the most creative mind must have looked about in vain for anything to feed fancy with in the acres of flat monotony which constituted the entire landscape between Netherlaw and Braidmoss. There were several small towns on the way — modified Netherlaws — and Braidmoss itself was a confusion of iron-works, factories, model houses for working-men, and gimcrack cottages.

In front of the Braidmoss station the Laighbield coach stood waiting. Its name was the 'Defiance.' It was high-wheeled, low-roofed, ill-ventilated, and narrow ; faded green cushions covered the seats, and straw

covered the bottom.   The top was freighted
with farmers, cattle dealers and cadgers.
Inside sat three women—our royal street
acquaintance, Mrs Gillespie, and two others
of like standing in the social scale.

Ursula shuddered.   It was dreadful to be
obliged to travel by such a vehicle and in
such company—dreadful !   But she had done
with fighting against her evil lot ; so in
bitter silence she accepted this final indignity
put by fate upon the Elvester.

Till the last moment it seemed as if the
nobler sex were to have no representative
within, but just as the driver was cracking
his whip, a man came past the station-house
in hot haste, and made for the ' Defiance.'
There was laughter from above, mingled
with shouts of, ' Tak' your braw leisure,
Mungo !' ' Weel dune you, Mungo !' ' Ye'll
be an unco heap the waur of this, Mungo !'
and so on.   But, heedless of these amenities,
the late comer pressed forward, scrambled
into the coach, and sat down on the same side
as the country women, opposite the Elvesters.

He was of uncertain age, and of medium
stature and of chubby form ; he had big wild
eyes, of the shade known to milliners as
French-white ; he had a pink smooth face,
and a thin crop of lank straw-coloured hair,
carefully arranged on each side of his full
glossy brow.   He was clad from neck to heel
in a snuff-tinted overcoat ; he was crowned
with a Glengarry bonnet ; he wore black
woollen gloves.   He was ignored by Mrs
Gillespie ; but the other two hailed him in a
friendly manner.   Then he greeted respec-
tively, as Mrs Hairshaw and Jeannie Gebbie,
and proceeded to remark that it had been a
very hard morning ; then, though nobody had
dissented, he added by way of confirmation,—

'Yes, yes, yes ; it *was* rather icily ; yes, it
was.'

Hereupon Slyboots, peering through a loop-
hole left for his convenience, caught the eye
of Mr Mungo Mauchline resting on him, and
not liking it, executed a remonstrative trill
with variations.   In the middle of this performance, Mr Mungo Mauchline blandly

remarked that cats always made him 'remember upon the ark-enemy of mankynd,'
and respectfully solicited Ulrica to 'topple
the veechus little four-foot out over the
windy ;' a suggestion, however, which fell
to the ground unnoticed.   Slyboots having
presently ceased his lay, Mr Mungo Mauchline indulged the ladies with a specimen of
his vocal talents, by lilting a few staves of
' I'm ower young to marry yet ;' but having
soon to collapse, he attributed his breakdown
to 'horseness occasioned by the condeetion
of the atmosphere.'

' Ye'll thole to pu' that window close up to
the tap, Mungo,' said Mrs Gillespie abruptly.
' I am fair fornent the draught o't, d'ye see ;
an' I hae gotten a wild hoast,' and in testimony of her assertion she coughed violently.

Luckily the hinge of the window was out
of repair, and would not do its office ; otherwise the whole party must have been nearly
stifled before reaching Laighbield. Mr Mungo
Mauchline, after vainly attempting to close
the window, fell into a fit of abstraction

Some weighty matter was evidently before
his mind. Suddenly he seemed to see light.
With an air of great good fellowship, he
exclaimed,—

' As sure as my name is Mr Mungo Mauchline, and if I am anny joodge of the weather,
this *is* a shuperfine day.'

There was really nothing special about the
day ; but Mr Mungo Mauchline objected to
undue familiarity ; and this was his way of
making known how he chose to be called.

' It's a geyan coorse day,' returned Mrs
Gillespie, in an injured tone ; thinking of the
effects of that draught upon her ' hoast.'

' Yes, there *is* a wind into it, I own,' granted
Mr Mungo Mauchline, as if the day were his,
and he responsible for the quality of it ; ' there
is a little wind into it too—nut a rantin',
tantin', tearin' wind ; but a nookin', soughin',
wurnin' wind, as the minister in the story says.'

' Jist a wheen claivers, a' thae stories aboot
ministers,' cried Mrs Gillespie tartly ; ' ministers is nane dafter nor ither folk, an' no sae
daft as some, Mungo.'

' I yield to no man in my respec' for the cloth,' rejoined Mr Mungo Mauchline. ' I am at all times ripe and ready for a confab with our most worthy cleric, I assure you. Last time I forgathered with him, says he to me, as friendly and confidential as you like—" Mr Mungo Mauchline, I see you are joost oot for your evening walk." '

'Gin that was a' he had to say, he micht as weel ha'e keepit it till himsel',' opened Mrs Gillespie snappishly.

' His most honoured lady was alongside,' continued Mr Mungo Mauchline, turning his conversation from Mrs Gillespie to her who sat next him; ' she was in full rank and unicorn, as the saying is—they would be for Baronshaugh, I joodge.'

' She's a gleg wee wifie yon,' rejoined Jeannie Gebbie, a rosy young matron, whose proper title was Mrs Andrew Hairshaw; but Laighbield had a fancy for continuing to call married women by the maiden name.

' She has the fine majestic swagger,' said Mr Mungo Mauchline admiringly.

'She's naething but an upsettin' cratur,' put in Mrs Gillespie, deeply scornful. 'But we're a' John Tamson's bairns; an' I haud mysel' as guid as her, I can tell ye—an' maybe a wee grain less ill-faured.'

'Ye ken,' said old Mrs Hairshaw, Jeannie Gebbie's mother-in-law, 'when the minister brocht hame his bride, the folk tell't that she wasna' to ca' bonnie, but that he maun ha'e been pleased wi' the airy gait o' her, an' the takin' turn.'

'Takin' turn,' echoed Mrs Gillespie; 'she has a tongue wad clip clouts. An' for complexion—she's black enough to mairch through the haill land o' Egypt, an' no a cur yelp the mair o't.'

'Hoot, she'll dae fine, ye'll see,' returned Mrs Hairshaw; 'the minister himsel' is by ordinar set on her.'

'Ou ay, ou ay! wise man's he is, he canna see the cat wink on Matilda, though she *should* skirl an' lauch in the verra kirk.'

'It's no true,' said Jeannie Gebbie warmly; 'she ne'er lauch in the kirk yet.'

'Weel, maybe no—clashes ay gets buttons an' tapes put to them as they gang—but sae they tell't me.'

'There's ay twa sets o' a tale, onyway,' replied Jeannie Gebbie, still warmly; an as weel ha'e the richt's the wrang o't: on Sawbath was a-week the minister swoopet wi' a preacher frae abune Auchterbrechan. *He* wasna nae bricht staur—'

'Wheesht, lassie!' interposed Mrs Hairshaw; 'he was a wee hue blate in oor muckle kirk, the bit chiel.'

'I doot he wadna been a sparkler nae gate, granny. I dinna like them 'ats fit to loup out ower the poopit—that's too muckle spunk; but yon ane had nane ava; nor I am no for them 'at dings an' bangs the guid Book a' to bits; but I wadna ha'e them staun like a stooky image, haudin' a grip o' the place on the paper a' the time. That was the way o' him; an', quo' he—'

'Hoot, toot, woman!' again interrupted the mother-in-law.

'Na, granny; ye maun let me speak up

for oor wee leddy,' persisted Jeannie. 'Quo
he, "Who can imagine or describe the
thoughts and feelings of a parent hen?"
an' wi' that, a young lassie the minister's wife
had aside her in the manse-pew, gied a kin'
o' chocket squeal o' a giggle. The minister's
wife hersel' didna say cheep, sae did she
na.'

Not being in a position to call this account
in question, Mrs Gillespie passed it over
without notice; but she waspishly remarked,—

'I wad be nane sweer to gi'e a screech
noo and than aboot hens mysel', and sae be
I was to mak' five or sax hunner a-year
by't.'

'It wasna a' ta'en up wi' hens,' said Jeannie
Gebbie; 'deed, no! it was unco wersh; an'
dreich, dreich, an' stappet fu' o' scriptur' texts
forby.'

'Some thinks,' quoth cheery Mrs Hairshaw—'an' I'll no presume to say they're
wrang—that a sermon wantin' texts is nae
better than brose would be wantin'
lumps.'

"Weel I wat then, granny, yon *was* the lumpy anes, an' sae frichtfu' lang. Our ain doctor's is like midges; but baith o' yon man's was like bum-bees.'

'You are correc' in your statements,' broke in Mr Mungo Mauchline, with an air of " it's my turn now." 'You are perfec'ly correc' in your statements. The cleric you allude to is not by anny means a startlesome preacher. I myself am in favour of a carnal discorse' (practical, he meant, likely) 'though at the same time I do not tottaly proheebit something wheech may jumble the joodgment and confound the understanding. But the fac' is this,—the clergy is too pharisetical, keeping their rostrum strictly from the laity, when, if they would only invite the intellectual members of their own congregation to deliver an address or so, from time to time, it would be a fine rest to themself, nut to mention a recreation to the people. The humble indiveedual you now behold, for instant, might not objec' occasionally to throw out a word.'

'I. wadna' be keen to expawtiate,' said
Mrs Hairshaw dissuasively. 'I wad haud
to the poetry, an' I was you, Mungo.'

'I could do something in the poytry line
over and above, mistress. My aim is to
projooce what is called an epic ; but I have
never yet exac'ly taken hold of my subjec',
so to speak. Of course, I turn off a trifle
now and again—for diversion, not for lucre ;
one I forwarded to the manse the other day,
with which I have every grounds for hopping
our worthy cleric's lady was highly gratified.
It was to this effec',—

> " Your kyindness, most respec'ed sir,
>   Forget it shall I never ;
>   How you sent my assistant James some bottles
>   of wine,
>   When he lay sick of fever."

But being of a private natture, I shupress the
remains. Nut long since I enclosed a lyric
to the *Cornrigshire Ghronicler.* The editor
was kynd enough to decline it with thanks—
with *thanks,* you notice ; *that* was flattering,
I think. The sonnet was entitled,—

Lines suggested by beholding a Steam-Engine.

"Saw you the steam-engine, that great iron-horse?
  Like a puffing Leviathan he purshues his corse.
  If into his way you ventured for to go,
  Oh friend! you would soon be laid very low.
  Just as when you go along in the morning,
  You may see a gay, gorgeous flower the side of the road
      adorning,
  But next day, when you pass in your early walk,
  There is nothing left but the bare stalk.
  A byke of bees would—"'

'Ne'er heed the hin'erend,' interrupted impatient Mrs Gillespie; 'we hinna nae skill o' poetry here ava; we gar the psaulms o' David ser' oor turn.'

'The loss is yours,' responded the bard; and he retired within himself, and gazed with rapt attention at the roof.

'You're unco quate noo, Mungo,' said Jeannie Gebbie, after a while.

'I may be cawing all the harder at the thinking,' he stiffly answered, and continued his roof-gazing.

'Some folk's sair saddlet wi' an ill temper,' observed Mrs Gillespie.

'Ne'er fash,' said pacific Mrs Hairshaw;
' it's nae suner on than it's aff.'

'An' it's nae suner aff than it's on,' retorted
Mrs Gillespie.

On the other side, meanwhile, there had
been silence. Miss Elvester had been study-
ing *Punch*, with amused interludes between
the pages, to give ear now to the 'poytry'
of Mr Mungo Mauchline, and now to his
no less singular prose. And, in point of
fact, these were being displayed at present
not for the sole edification of the country-
women to whom they were addressed, but
chiefly for the sake of the distinguished-
looking strangers opposite. Mr Mungo
Mauchline, well up in Laighbield gossip, had
made a correct guess at the identity of the
sisters ; and he was particularly anxious that
the ladies of the Brae should now understand
that they were travelling in company with
one who was no common man indeed, although his state were mean. And he did
succeed in impressing both Miss Elvester
and Ulrica with his out-of-the-wayness,—

though whether in the way he intended, is another question.

But Ursula never noticed him; Ursula sat with her eyes down, thinking her own thoughts, and so would have remained till the end of the journry, had not in process of time the name ‘Berwick’ suddenly penetrated her self-absorption, and against her will compelled her to attention.

‘Ay, Donal’ Berwick’s to be settled in the Auchterbrechan Laigh Kirk syne,’ Mrs Hairshaw was saying. ‘Keep me! I mind Donal’ a wee, sonsie, curly-heided callant, speerin the won’erfu’est questions that ever could be, and ettlen’ to ken the oots and ins o’ ilka mortal thing. I had my ain fricht aboot the laddie when he was awa’ amang a’ thae throughither college chaps; for he was a gey speerity ane himsel’, an’ he was jist at the pairtin’ o’ the ways—between the tinin’ an’ the winnin’, as ye may speak. But I hear he has turned oot extraordinary; an’ a gran’ preacher, tae, they tell me that should ken.’

Mrs Gillespie hurried in as usual with her wet-blanket.

'I see nae gran' preachin' in't,' she said contemptuously ; 'he leuks on !'

'But he's nane o' your *slavish* readers,' observed Jeannie Gebbie. 'He hasna to kep the place wi' his finger, like that hankerin' ane wi' "the parent hen" ; as his Auntie Jean says, he comes awa wi't just beautiful.'

'Beautiful, beautiful !' sneered Mrs Gillespie ; 'trust his Auntie Jean for turning the best side o' Donal' to the sun.'

'Jean Berwick is a fine, canty body. Auld Scroggiehillock is unco fain to get her for his second ; but you'll no be for believin' that.'

'I'll believe't weel enough ; gin ye ha'e grippet thegether a wheen bawbees, it's no ill to buy yoursel' a bit man,' carped the female cynic.

Mr Mungo Mauchline having at length sufficiently acquainted himself with the roof decorations, came out of his pet with the remark,—

'I have the best grounds for stating that Miss Jean Berwick has no present intention of altering her condeetion of life.'

'I wadna lippen her wi' the chance,' said Mrs Gillespie pointedly.

'I joodge Miss Jean to be a speciment of firm tenicity of opeenion,' was the rejoinder. Forby that, if she *was* to lay her mind to matrimony, she would certainly look for a shuitable partner, nut a patriarch hovering on the brink of the sepulchre.'

'Sepulchre or nae sepulchre, there's braw need o' some haimert-like body at Scroggiehillock,' said Mrs Gillespie, who always shifted her position when likely to be foiled in argument; 'for o' a' the hooses I ha'e ever seen, yon is the likest a Marymass Saturday.' (Marymass Saturday was the yearly fair at Leighbield, and Mrs Gillespie's simile meant to imply that the house spoken of presented an aspect of disorder sickening to contemplate.) 'The donnert auld fule has put yon youngest dochter o' his to a boardin'-schule—to learn manners, nae less,' she continued, with a satirical laugh. ' But, losh ! he needna fash his heid ; sen' a cauf to Lunnon, it'll come hame a coo.'

' You make me recollec' upon a good storry,' said Mr Mungo Mauchline. ' There was once a worthy minister in the north, and one Sabbath day, says he, in his discorse, " I warn all here, wheech make free with mince-oaths—Losh, gosh, and— " '

' You mind me o' something tae,' interposed Mrs Gillespie, in accents of asperity. ' You mind me o' the college fallow whase heid was swelled wi' knowledge, for yours is swelled wi' weanly stories, Mungo.'

The unappreciated story-teller once more subsided, and thoughtfully fumbled for a while in his great-coat pockets. By-and-by he produced a rumpled envelope, carefully smoothed it out, spread it on his knee, and read, with particular emphasis on the first word,—

' *Mr* Mungo Mauchline, postmaster, Laighbield, Cornrigshire.'

This instructive ceremony over, he re-

turned the envelope to his pocket, and after
another search, brought to light a blue paper
bag, which, when with grave deliberateness it
had been opened up, he held towards Ulrica,
with the 'hop' that he might use the freedom of proffering her 'a few cocoa-nut
chips.'

But Ulrica declined the kindness.

'A most innocent little condiment,' urged
Mr Mungo Mauchline ; 'no plaister of Paris,
I assure you.   Do not be feared to deprive
me of the goodies, little lady ; I have plenty
more at home.'

Nevertheless Ulrica would not be tempted ;
so the possessor of the cocoa-nut chips had to
bestow these innocent little condiments upon
tart Mrs Gillespie and blythe Jeannie Gebbie.

The girls were not sorry when they at last
received the intelligence that an end was
near.   The coach was passing under an
archway of nearly leafless trees, before a
pair of high wide gates, which admitted to
an avenue, which led through the policies
which surrounded the mansion of the Laird

of Laighbield.   When Miss Elvester told
her sisters that this was Baronshaugh, they,
on account of the connection between Cassillis the laird and Christian's Netherlaw
protectress, turned their eyes with considerable interest towards the grey, dignified old
house seen far away, and continued their
scrutiny till an abrupt turn in the road hid it
from view.   Baronshaugh left behind, they
went over a low, broad bridge, by kirk and
manse, down a narrow lane, into a broad,
winding, and very irregularly-constructed
street, up to 'The Cassillis Arms,' the
terminus.

CHAPTER IX.

LAIGHBIELD.

'Having through all the village past,
To a small cottage came at last.'

THE little country town (its own
people called it a town, other
people called it a village) lay
snugly sheltered as in the bottom of a cup;
and the land forming the sides of this cup
was richly agricultural, as it is the specialty
of Cornrigshire land to be. Baronshaugh
had an imposing aspect; the parish manse
also was dignified in its degree; but there
was nothing else imposing or dignified about
Laighbield. Not the Established Church,
though it certainly held its head pretty high;

not the Free Church, though it prided itself
upon the fact that the laird and his mother
were members of it ; not their United Pres-
byterian rival, though that was flourishing as
any green bay tree ; and still less the showy
new bank and the far from showy old Masons'
Hall.   These were the only public buildings
in the place, excepting Mr Langbiggin's
bonnet factory at the mouth of the Wynd,
that lane through which the stage-coach had
to pass on entering the town.

The Laighbield housewife was thought of
small account indeed who did not, in addition
to her ordinary domestic duties, earn a considerable sum weekly ; and machinery not
having then, as it has since, taken the place
of hand-work in this branch of industry, all
through the little town were to be seen women
knitting Prince Charlies, deer-stalkers, Glen-
garries, and so on, with perfectly magical
rapidity ; and this over and above what was
done in the aforesaid factory, which employed
most of the girls of the district, and many of
the men as well.

At the ringing of the six o'clock bell, the workers began to appear about the street. The girls wore dark drugget skirts and aprons, light calico 'short-gowns,' and long scarf-like plaids, arranged about the head and shoulders by way of a wimple, both ends falling loosely over one arm; and had they but believed it, they looked out of comparison nicer so, than in the Sunday finery in which their hearts delighted.

'Dressers' and knitters, and every straggler and idler, 'glowered' with undisguised curiosity at the three strangers walking up their town. Miss Elvester was calmly impervious, and Ursula haughtily so. But poor Ulrica grew more and more seriously discomposed. And matters reached a climax, when she heard her golden locks described by one loud-voiced critic as 'a pickle tow,' and her undulating gait compared by another to the rocking of a 'craddle.' But school board education was in the future then; it is therefore quite open to us to believe, that any stranger visiting Laighbield in the present day, would have a greatly improved state of manners to report.

Opposite the complaisant little U. P. church, between a weaver's shop and the town pump, a broad road known as the Brigend, struck away from the main street to the right. Turning down here, Miss Elvester and her girls came once more upon the river, which they had crossed near the gates of Baronshaugh, and had lost sight of since. A second bridge brought them to a road bordered with lime-trees, banked and hedged on the one hand, on the other looking down to the stream, and across that to stretches of garden, and a meadow, and a meal mill. At the end of the lime-tree road they had again to part company with the river; and this time it was to turn into a grassy lane, which led between clover parks, right up one side of the cup whose hollow contained Laighbield.

A tiny house on the height above them was their future home. It looked as unpretentious as could be; but there was a pleasing effect about it, scarcely to be described. It seemed so in harmony with its surroundings, that it might have grown up amidst them as the trees had grown. Honeysuckle climbed the walls; willows shaded the gables; a few late flowers still bloomed in front, protected by a thick laurel hedge; a rowan tree stood at each side of the rustic gate—to ward off witchcraft.

Ursula said not a word; but her face assumed an expression of relief. It was not for nothing that she had lived so many weeks in a flat in Chapel Street: *this* was certainly a very great improvement upon *that.* So also thought Ulrica.

'Oh, the gem! the little nest!' she cried, mixing her metaphors.

'But the rooms are few and small,' said Miss Elvester; 'and a state of woeful upsidedownness they must be in to-day. Be prepared to find the house piled roof-high with packing boxes.'

This warning had no sooner been pronounced than the door was opened, and the Elvesters—once of Eastravoe—entered the Brae.

CHAPTER X.

A ROUND PEG IN A SQUARE HOLE.

She is too low for a high praise, too brown for a fair praise, and too little for a great praise.

MIDWAY between the bonnet factory at the mouth of the Wynd and the east gates of Baronshaugh, were the ivy-grown walls which surrounded the parish manse. Within these walls, looking forth from the bay window of a bright and pleasant breakfast-parlour, on the fine variety of flowering shrubs which beautified the grounds, waited, about eight o'clock on an early November day, a dark little—girl, was she? in a white and crimson morning-gown. Girl she was none; girlish as she seemed, she

was a wife of several years' standing. She
was no beauty (had not the tawniness of
her complexion passed into a proverb in
the town ?) ; but she possessed a peculiarly
piquant face, shaded by a profusion of the
softest, waviest, brownest hair, and lit up
by a pair of saucy dark eyes, in which
ever lurked a laugh ; yet behind the laugh
were great possibilities in the way of
pathos too.

The pen hesitates, unwilling to record it ;
only it may as well be confessed at once,
this lady was far from being the ideal of
a pastor's wife. Nobody would for one
moment have thought of holding her up
as ' an ensample to the flock ; ' nor was
she that sort of person upon whose tomb-
stone would one day be carved the en-
comium, ' Beloved by all who knew her.'
Alas, no ! not even the large charity of
grave-yard literature would dare so great
a deflection from fact as that. But nega-
tive criticism is unsatisfactory ; you want
to know what she was rather than what

she was not.   Assume as lenient a frame
of feeling as is possible to you, then, and
you shall judge.

The man who was being waited for presently came in.   He was a grave, scholarly
personage, about the prime of life; and
he was singularly unlike the husband anybody would have imagined for that elf in
the gay morning gown.   At his entrance,
the lady turned from the window.

'At last!' she exclaimed.   'Does Dr
Brackenburn realise that he has kept his
household waiting fully ten minutes?   Was
there a paragraph to finish when the bell
rang?'

'Something of the sort,' he said.   'I beg
your pardon, Matilda.'

'Which I grant,' she replied, 'because
I have found you to be in the main a
punctual man, even in spite of paragraphs.
Isn't it Byron who says that a woman should
never be seen eating?—she should never
confess either, that she wants to eat, I
suppose; but I am as hungry as a hunter

Alan; so let prayers be short this morning, please.'

Yet, when the couple did sit down to breakfast, the lady was a vast deal more interested in her husband's plate than in her own. She marked with growing dissatisfaction how the morning's letters were usurping that attention properly due to the morning's meal; and when she could contain herself no longer, she stole silently round the table and blindfolded Dr Brackenburn, by clasping her hands over his eyes.

'Now, then,' she said, 'tell me what you have before you—apples of Sodom or saw-dust?'

'Game pie, is it not?'

'Actually!' said she, returning to her place. 'Well, do try to look a little as if you appreciated your mercies. It outrages one's feelings, as a housekeeper, to see you so indifferent to creature comforts. Alan, did my eyes deceive me, or is the letter in your hand from our dear but erring brother of Braidmoss?'

The glance that she received in reply caused her to inquire with a wicked smile,—

'Is it venial or mortal sin that I've committed this time?'

As there was no answer, she went on,—

'Dear, you must forgive me, that ever since hearing him call somebody who wasn't orthodox about the sun and moon standing still that day over the valley of Ajalon, "Our dear but erring brother," I can't leave off so nicknaming your co-presbyter of Braidmoss. But is the letter from the Rev. Daniel Carnegy, M.A.?'

'The note is from Carnegy,' her husband answered; 'it is merely about pulpit supply, my dear.'

'And where is Mr Carnegy now?—still pretty near Paradise, of course—but geographically-speaking, I mean?'

'He writes from Belfast.'

'Then he must be visiting the bride's uncles, those descendants of the Irish kings that we have heard so much about. Poor bride!—I beg your pardon—happy, happy bride, I should have said. I wish I could know how Mr Carnegy proposed to her. I can fancy him droning in tones like the concentrated essence of the tune Coleshill,—"Oh woman greatly beloved, be my fond partner through this vale of tears."'

'Nonsense, my dear.'

'I have strong premonitions of unpleasantness, Alan. Mrs Carnegy will be forewarned by her husband that I am an earthen vessel; for though Mr Carnegy is what people of his school call "a consecrated man;" he isn't incapable of a fine, full-flavoured aversion.'

'I suspect the aversion is on the other side, Matilda.'

'Not the monopoly. Do you think I can't tell when people don't like me?'

'What I think is, that you take no trouble at all to make people like you, but the contrary. It still seems to be with you as of old,—"Love me, if you dare!"'

At that she coloured a little. Then, with a laugh, she asked,—

'Should you be greatly glad to see your
wife a world's favourite, Alan ?'

'To see her much less than that would
greatly gladden me.'

'Then I must try what can be done.
When we call at Braidmoss manse, I'll
astonish you.'

"If you intend any mischief, I refuse to
go with you to Braidmoss manse at all.'

'What do you mean by "mischief" ?'

'Anything like a repetition of what we
had yesterday, for instance.'

'When the delicious Mr Langbiggin was
here ? Oh, Alan, you *know* the man hadn't
the dawn of an idea that I was quizzing
him. And I had to find some escape for
my feelings, when I heard the rich bonnet
manufacturer accusing the poor minister of
unreasonableness. Mr M'Spur has peti-
tioned the session for an addition to his
manse ; but Mr Langbiggin says that there
are seven apartments in the Free Church
manse, and wants to know what a minister
(not like a mercantile gentleman at all !)

would do with more. So the mercantile
gentleman must build a house nearly as big
as Baronshaugh for himself and niece; but
Mr M'Spur, who has a wife and ten children, ought to be humble and thankful in
seven apartments!'

'I can only say, my dear, that you took
a most extraordinary way of advancing Mr
M'Spur's interests.'

'But, Alan, we've rather wandered from
the point, haven't we? It was the call at
Braidmoss manse we were at. This is how
I'll make myself appreciated there: I will be
as artless as the cat when she has designs
on the cream-pot; I will bring out my entire
stock of moralities thus, calling Braidmoss
"this corner of the vineyard," and the Established Church "our Zion;" assuring the
bride that I consider her husband's preaching
to be "very refreshing" (which, indeed, I
don't); remarking that the flock at Braidmoss
is not only fed, but feasted on the finest of
the wheat, and that no other labourer divides
the word with such great acceptance as does

Mr Carnegy; and winding up with the hope
that Mr Carnegy and myself may have many
sweet and precious hours of edifying com-
munion in times to come.   I think all that
has the right "sough" about it.   Mr Carnegy will hail me as a prodigal returned—
what did you say, Alan?'

He had not said anything; but he now
observed quietly,—

'You are in what, I presume, you call a witty
vein this morning; but I have prejudices, you
know; don't you think it would be only kind
on your part to respect these a little?'

'Forgive me, forgive me, dear; and I
won't be witty any more to-day.   But I
wasn't mocking at anything sacred, only at
pious slang and maudle.   Why must some
good people fly to metaphor whenever re-
ligion is the theme?'

'Why, I might echo, must some other
people fly to metaphor, no matter what the
theme is?'

'*Tu quoque* does not settle an argument,
Dr Brackenburn.'

'But it sometimes silences an arguer,' was the reply.

And that, apparently, was what Dr Brackenburn wished to do; for immediately afterwards, breakfast being over, he would have left the room. His wife, however, interposed her tiny person between the door and him, saying,—

'Pray, oh pray, not yet. Is it fair that all the parish should have more of you than I, whose right is the greatest here?'

At that reproach, he turned back and sat down again.

'I am to blame,' he said. 'I too often forget what a young thing you are still, and how dull your present life is as contrasted with your girlhood.'

'I don't complain of my present life,' she answered. 'I know how to amuse myself (though you don't always approve); and there is only one small blessing I sometimes fret for—a little more of your society.'

'If that be all, you need not remain unsatisfied; my study is not far to seek.'

'But when I seek your study, I know that I am disturbing you, and putting to flight fine trains of beautifully-linked ideas. And I am ashamed to call you away from among the isms and ologies to listen to my small-beer chronicles. I wish I were a learned woman, dear, who could follow and appreciate the abstruse articles you write for those reviews, and who could discuss metaphysics with you, and Comte and Schossenhauer, and the higher criticism.'

'I think I on the whole prefer you as you are,' replied the husband, smiling.

Thus encouraged, the lady went and seated herself on the grave doctor's knee, and put her arms about his neck. And then she laughed, and said,—

'A learned woman would never be capable of fooling like this ; would she, Alan ?'

'I cannot tell. You know one of the species—ask her.'

'What! Mrs Inverarity ? Oh no ; I am holding aloof from her just now. She is writing a book on the Ten Lost Tribes, and if I were to venture near she would inflict every word of her tediousness upon me.'

' I am afraid you hold very much aloof from all your friends, Matilda, and that without their being any writing of books in the question.'

' My friends—who are they ? '

' Your acquaintances, if you prefer it.'

' We have nothing in common ; no fellow-feelings to make us wondrous kind. I don't care a straw for any of them.'

' I must have been mistaken, then ; but I was under the impression that, much as you object to Langbiggin himself, you did like that quiet little niece of his.'

' But I don't *dis*like her, is as much as can be said. There is no peg in her to hang up a liking on ; she is neutral, conventional, commonplace.'

' She is a young lady who, I am very sure, will never say an unkind thing.'

' Nor ever do a kind one,' retorted Mrs Brackenburn. ' But, thank you, Alan ; I stand reproved. Let me tell you, however,

that Katie Langbiggin never criticises, only
because she never observes.   She is colour-
blind where shades of character are concerned.   There is an exasperating absence
of spontaniety about her, too.   I believe,
when she was a little child, some fairy god-
mother gave her a casket filled with neat
cut-and-dry remarks, and bade her through
life use no other ; so always, when she needs
to speak, she brings out the appropriate sen-
tences as they are wanted, then folds them
nicely up, and puts them back till they shall
be required again.'

'Well, there is Mrs M'Spur ; her conversation has colour enough and spontaneity
enough to please, I should imagine.'

'Her colour is used only to blacken everybody in Laighbield except Mr M'Spur and
the ten children.   But to go on with my
friends, there is Grizzel Cochrane—a good
girl, I know, only so obtrusively beamingly
complacent always, that I can't help wanting
to see her in a little distress, just as a healthy
variety.   And last on the list, ecclesiastical

Mrs Cassillis, whose weekly drawing-room prayer-meeting is a fortuitous concourse of atoms, for the assembly is confused, and the more part knows it is come together. The last time I attended it, a demure maiden lady prayed that "we here present might so walk, *as* that all men seeing, should follow after us." That wasn't quite so proper, was it?'

'My dear,' said her husband seriously, 'it is always painful to listen to a woman's disparagement of women. Cannot you leave it to men to point out your weaknesses? It is a task in which they need no help from any of yourselves.'

'Don't I know it well! From Adam onward, the great creatures have never let slip a chance of casting in our teeth what poor things we are. But I will not own myself a traitress. I have not been bringing any really damaging charges against the sisterhood; and, indeed, if you want my opinion, it is that, with all our spite and littleness—which we hear so much and so often about—

we rank in heaven's sight quite as high at
least as you.   Our faults are certainly more
irritating to each other than your faults are
to us ; yet we can admire each other too.
The feeling one of us bears to another who
is high above her is a feeling not under-
standed of men.   For my own part,
whenever I come in contact with a really
noble woman, I almost want to worship
her.'

'Why not be a really noble woman yourself ?' it was very gently put to her.

'If you but realised what it costs me to be
even such as I am, you would spare the question,' she replied.   'Yes ; I take fits of trying to be nice—or estimable, at any rate—
and I get on wonderfully for a while.   But
then, just as I begin to imagine that there is
only a pasteboard partition between me and
perfection, I stumble, and fall headlong from
my pedestal ; and so being once more
"among the pots," as the psalm says, I
have it out for all my former self-denial,
and perfectly revel in the blackness.   Oh,

it is ever the old story—but I've told you it all before, Alan.'

'Never mind that ; tell it to me again, if it seems to do you good.'

'Long ago I used to make periodical re-solutions to get up early to study. I would do grandly for a time. Then must come a morning when, instead of springing as soon as called, I would choose to have five minutes more of luxury. That meant fall-ing asleep again, of course. But do you imagine that I, who had meant to be up with the sun, would rise when I was again wakened—this time by the break-fast bell—not I ! At such times I gener-ally spent the most of the forenoon in bed.'

'Those in authority over you should not have suffered it. But, tell me, are you in one of those better moods to-day ? I ask with a purpose.'

'That's alarming! What is expected of me, pray ?'

'Some poor people stand in need of you.

You have heard of them before, you may remember.'

'Yes; and I have kept sending whatever has been required.'

'I want you to go now, not to send.'

'Oh, what misery! I would rather hear the MS. of "The Ten Lost Tribes" from beginning to end, or the longest sermon of the most confirmed platitudinarian in your presbytery! I should not like parish visiting.'

'But are we in this world to do only what we like?'

'I don't believe we can be intended to do what we emphatically feel we have no vocation for.'

'Until you have given a thing of this sort a fair trial, you cannot say you have no vocation for it. You once believed you had no vocation for teaching, yet now you get on famously with your class.'

'That is because my boys have come to like me somehow.'

'Doubtless; and your boys' mothers would

also come to like you, if you cared about the matter.'

'Would they? Ah, I must tell you an anecdote illustrative of a boy's mother. One of my dearest disciples was repeating the first Psalm, and he persisted in having it, " Nor sitteth in the *corner* chair." I tried to get him to see that there could be no harm in a corner chair,—that when a boy was sent to the corner in disgrace, the evil was all in himself, none of it in the corner. Then I went on,—" It is a *scorner's* chair that is spoken of here. Who can tell us what a scorner is ?" Immediately Tommy Gillespie's hand went out. "Well," said I, "what is he ?" Tommy's answer was rather startling,—" It's no' a he, it's a she : *yoursel's* the scorner, mem !" I nearly laughed, though I looked as stern as I could, and asked Tommy what he meant ? But " My mither tell't us," was all the satisfaction I could gain. Such is my character in Laighbield. They make out a sad case against me, Alan.'

'They don't know you ; and you are precisely the person who, seen only on the surface, is sure to be misjudged.   That is partly why I am anxious that you should go among the people a little ; partly also because there is crying need for some kindly, active woman to make her influence felt in Laighbield.'

‘ But if the kindly active woman have not tact ? I feel no aptitude for being a Sister of Mercy.'

‘ The aptitude may come with the occasion for it.'

‘ Very well ;—please the Fates, you shall have your way.   And is there anything else disagreeable that you can think of for me to do ? I may as well be thorough.   Might I not take a missionary tour through the Netherlaw Reformatory, for example ?'

‘ You had better, I think, confine your energies to the parish.'

‘ I have promised to energise in the parish, then, but not to-day.   To-day I must call at the Brae, and make myself as charming as I can to those Elvesters,—and after, I am promised at Auchterbrechan.   Miss Berwick

has got the manse in order, but she wants
me to do the finishing touches. By the way,
Alan, I've been thinking that I must find a
wife for Mr Berwick.'

'That is a finding most men prefer to
undertake for themselves.'

'Which is a pity; they so often choose
unwisely, and rue ever after.'

Saying which, Mrs Brackenburn looked
up with an indescribable half-comic, half-
pathetic expression, as if asking, between
jest and earnest, 'Is it not so with you?'
but the eyes that met hers must have perfectly satisfied her that her husband was far
enough from rueing the unwisdom of his
choice.

'I have fixed on Katie Langbiggin for
the minister-elect of Auchterbrechan,' she
announced, after a pause.

'What! the young lady who is so neutral
—so uninteresting?'

'And why not? Men and women judge
differently; and I don't know that a man
likes a woman any the less that her mind

resembles a sheet of unused blotting-paper, and is all ready to become a fainter copy of his own.'

'And if Donald Berwick and you are satisfied, nothing else is wanted, I suppose, —not such an unimportant item as the lady's concurrence, for example.'

'If she should not concur, I shall have to turn elsewhere. But don't take alarm; I meditate nothing which you could not perfectly approve of. I simply intend to give the pair every opportunity of finding out for themselves that they were made for each other. Ah, but I should like to see Mr Berwick in love; it would amuse me more than anything I can think of to see the handsome giant blushing and stammering under a girl's glance! But I've set my heart upon this thing, chiefly because of my fellow-feeling with the licentiate who a few Sundays ago interested us in the anxieties of a parent hen. On every subject I tried that young man, but found him blank. In sheer despair I stumbled haphazard on the

question,—" Mr Mucklewham, are you sentimental ? " That roused him. He grasped
at the idea as if it were the elixir of life, or
perpetual motion, or any of the other things
men have gone mad trying to discover, and
with a fervency I couldn't a moment before
have conceived him capable of, ejaculated,
" *Real* sentimental ! " So I, too, am *real*
sentimental, though not one in Laighbield,
I know, would credit it,—or if any did, they
would put it down to me for a crime; for what
I do is a fault, and what I don't do is a fault,
and if I have no fault they manufacture one.
I am a much-to-be-commiserated woman,
Alan ; I am a round peg in a square hole.'

This was true enough, unfortunately ; and
the result of Mrs Brackenburn's first attempt
at parish work — for she did go out and
energise, though not that day — was an
anonymous billet, addressed to ' Dr Brackenburn's Meddlesome Matty,' and containing
the following pointed satire :—

> ' Sometimes she'd lift the teapot-lid, to peep at what was
>   in it,
> Or tilt the kettle, if you did but turn your back a minute.'

'Withdraw thy foot from thy neighbour's house, lest he become weary of thee, and so hate thee.'

The minister's wife showed this production to all her friends, and made much fun of it; but if in public she laughed, in secret, I think, she cried a little too.

CHAPTER XI.

MÒNCRIEFF.

'I know a maiden fair to see,
Take care !
She can both false and friendly be,
Beware ! beware !'

THE first acquaintances Christian made after she had gone to seek her fortunes as a governess were Dugald and Moncrieff Urquhart, nephew and niece by marriage of Mrs Cassillis of Argyll Gardens. Mr Urquhart's place, Craigie Urquhart, was in the neighbourhood of Braidmoss; and as Dugald had no town-house of his own, he and his sister made themselves very much at home in their Aunt Marjorie's, and both stayed

there days and weeks at a stretch, as
often as it suited them.

The brother was rather over thirty—emphatically fine-looking, in the hairdresser's-
model style of perfection, a landed pro-
prietor, and a marrying man. Conscious of
so much greatness, he set high value upon
his person ; indeed, Sir Roland de Vane was
carelessness itself on the bridal question
compared to Mr Urquhart.

The sister was one-and-twenty, and an
acknowledged belle.   But if Nature had
generously given to Moncrieff a fair face,
Fortune had stingily withheld from her a
full purse ; her entire income, she would
many a time complain, was barely sufficient
to keep her in gloves alone.

This young lady soon grew very friendly
with Willie Ruthven's governess ; and Christian had the privilege of becoming acquainted
with Miss Urquhart's whole history—with
the long list of her adorers — with the
flowery catalogue of compliments paid to
her by these.   No confidence was expected

in return. That would have bored Moncrieff. She had no interest in her neighbours' concerns, as such ; her fellow-creatures
and their affairs she took cognisance of only
in so far as they stood in relation to her own
personality ; and she was absolutely devoid
of the imagination, or gift, or grace, which
might have enabled her to put herself, though
but for one moment, in anybody else's place.
But if the one girl were pleased to be auto-
biographical, and if the others were content
to listen to autobiography, that was their
own business.

In close connection with her master theme
—self, Moncrieff had a great deal to say
about her two cousins, Quentin Cassillis of
Baronshaugh, and Captain Glen Cassillis, of
Her Majesty's —th foot ; but from all
her multiplication of words, the only defi-
nite notion to be extracted came to this—
both one and the other were steadfast
admirers of Miss Urquhart.

Early in December Captain Cassillis was
expected home, and for his better enter-

tainment during the visit his cousin came
to spend a fortnight at Argyll Gardens.
Mrs Cassillis was laid up with some slight
temporary illness; but no matter, Moncrieff
would receive Glen, and do the honours to
his fullest satisfaction.

On the evening preceding the day on
which Captain Cassillis was to arrive, there
was a grand orchestral concert in the Town
Hall. Moncrieff went, of course; not for the
music's sake certainly—who cared for orchestral music?—but, as she went to church, for
instance, because it formed part of the re-
cognised programme.

And while Moncrieff was thus sacrificing
inclination on the altar of conventionality,
Christian was suffering from a sharp attack
of home-sickness. She had no cause to be
unhappy in Netherlaw, but the reverse.
Her pupil was her pet and her plaything;
everybody was civil to her, and she received even more than ordinary kindness
from Mrs Cassillis. Yet there were times,
as now, when she longed to be with her own

people, and felt as if she could not live
another day apart from Jenny. Driving
through the town one afternoon, she had
caught a passing glimpse of Mr and Mrs
Rich of Bresta, and this fit of home-sickness
was the result. She had bravely striven
against it, and, so far, had been successful
in at least keeping appearances up. But
now, being left to herself, she became worse
and worse, until it seemed that nothing short
of a hearty cry would do her any good. That
weakness, however, she would not indulge in,
so went to the piano instead, that she might,
if it were possible, sing melancholy away.
But, no ! the sound of her own voice brought
tears to her eyes at once, and she had to give
up the experiment. Light literature might
serve the purpose better. She would try that.
And ready to hand lay a novel, on the couch
where Moncrieff had lately been reclining.

Miss Urquhart was a great reader, after
her sort ; that is, she would rush through the
realms of fiction at the rate of three volumes
an afternoon, and with about the same

measure of appreciation as travellers by
night express have of the country through
which they pass. What Moncrieff had last
been running over was a work which Christian knew by name, and remembered, because reviewers had unanimously condemned
it ; had even, some of them, entreated
British women not to look at it. Well, here
it was, open in her hand, and so, in spite
of reviewers' warnings, this British woman
did look at it. One half-page she scanned ;
no more—that was enough. The very hot
love-scene, in the thick of which she had
lighted, did not attract—it repelled her—and
vexed with herself for having so much as
opened the book, she let it drop from her
fingers as if it had been a loathly thing, and
lifted her face to encounter a pair of keen,
dark eyes, whose owner had just drawn aside
the curtains which hung in the pillared archway between the front and back drawing-
rooms.

' Miss Elvester, I believe,' said the
stranger, bowing.

Thus taken by surprise, and caught in the very act of reading that banned volume, Christian fell into some confusion, and answered to her name after a fashior highly annoying to herself.

'And I am Glen Cassillis,' said the in truder. And he begged the young lady's pardon for having startled her, and explained that some sudden alteration of arrangements had occasioned his coming on to Netherlaw a night earlier than he had intended. While a few generalities were being exchanged, Captain Cassillis, without thinking what he was about, lifted the book which he had seen fall from Christian's hand. Had it been any collection of moral tales, or manual of instructive reading, the man would never have touched it ; but being what it was, it could not, of course, be let alone.

Christian's face grew hot, when Captain Cassillis turned his glance to it from the title-page. She was angry, both with him and with herself—for what right had he to look at her like that ?—and she who had done no

wrong, whose conscience was perfectly clear.
Why, why must she so foolishly colour under
his satirical eyes? As for him, he confined
the satire to those eyes.

'An interesting story, isn't it?' he said,
in the most matter-of-fact tone.

'I don't think so—I mean I haven't read
it, and can't say,' she replied, with as much
dignity as she was mistress of.

But the previous flush, and the amended
sentence were against her, and then she
immediately afterwards excused herself, and
went away, Captain Cassillis was left thinking,—

'So much, then, for my mother's paragon;
but what a pity that falsehood should be
spoken in so singularly sweet a tone.'

On coming into the breakfast-room next
morning, Christian found Miss Urquhart and
Captain Cassillis there before her. She was
about to take the place which the present
indisposition of Mrs Cassillis left vacant at
table, when,—

'I'll save you the trouble, Miss Elvester,'

said Moncrieff, stepping in before her, and
sitting down.

'Thank you very much,' replied Christian,
quietly moving round to the side seat.

Upon which Captain Cassillis, thinking of
Thackeray's women, who scratch each other's
face in private, but are all affection to each
other in the sight of men, came to his own
conclusions ; and these were again unfavourable to his mother's paragon.

The beautiful Moncrieff was in great force,
and, not being one to waste her table-talk on
a woman, if a man were by, spoke right on
with her soldier-cousin, to the almost total
exclusion of the unfortunate third. Captain
Cassillis more than once attempted to bring
Christian in ; ineffectually, however, since she
made no effort to take the ball so thrown to
her, but always allowed Moncrieff to catch it
up again, and bear it away. This morning
Christian neither cared to be spoken to, nor
to speak. She knew that she had made a
bad impression, that she was disapproved of ;
and the consciousness vexed her to an absurd

degree, reducing her to the uncomfortable
state in which one is constantly obliged to
pause in one's employments to inquire—
' What is amiss with me ? '

Such a thing as this had never happened
to her before ; and it fretted her the more, to
think that the opinion of an entire stranger
should have the power of fretting her at
all.

In the course of the forenoon she was in
the back drawing-room, guiding Willie Ruthven's fingers over the scales, when the cousins
passed through.

' *You* don't instruct yourself in that kind,
do you ? ' said a voice, not meant for Christian's ears.

Christian heard, nevertheless, and knew
quite well what ' kind ' was alluded to.

' Not I, indeed,' responded Moncrieff,
lightly. ' It isn't my book, you know ; it is
Miss Elvester's.'

' Well, don't read it, or any other like
it,' said Glen ; and the pair passed out of
hearing.

In a short while Moncrieff reappeared alone.

'Did you hear how nearly I got into disgrace with cousin Glen?' she asked, coming up behind Christian.

'I heard,' said Christian, speaking coldly— how could she help it? 'and heard you tell your cousin that the book was mine.'

Moncrieff laughed.

'Wasn't it a bright thought?' she inquired, with great glee.

'Oh! I must be excused, if I don't quite appreciate the brightness of it.'

'It isn't a bit nice of Glen to go poking into things,' said Moncrieff. 'Do *you* think it is, Miss Elvester?'

'It is no business of mine to think anything about it (B flat, Willie, and third finger); only, if it is such a dreadful fault to read the book, it seems a little hard that I should be supposed to have done so.'

'Oh, it isn't dreadful at all! And I had to say something, hadn't I? Cousin Glen is so absurdly particular about me—you've no notion.'

'That must be very flattering,' said Christian.

'Do you think so? I call it tiresome and inconvenient. (Go on, Willie Ruthven; don't stare at me.) Of course, Miss Elvester, you won't make mischief; nobody would be so ill-natured as to make mischief between cousin Glen and me.'

'I am no mischief-maker, Miss Urquhart. But don't, please, do anything else that you mean to be ashamed of; because I'm afraid I shall not want to take any more upon my shoulders for some time.'

'Nothing—nothing more,' replied Moncrieff; and away she went, satisfied.

It is perhaps putting it too strongly to affirm that ugliness is the fault the most rigorously treated by men; but it certainly is not going too far to say that falsehood, when uttered by lips that are lovely, seems robbed of a measure of its shame. And Moncrieff possessed this great advantage of beauty. Their was an airy frankness about her besides, and an unshaken confidence in the obligation of everybody around her to do just exactly as she desired they should. So beauty, frankness, and confidence together, attained the gratifying result, that whoever else's projects might be thwarted, Miss Urquhart's were always triumphantly carried through.

CHAPTER XII.

MARRING HER FORTUNE.

Where're you find 'the cooling western breeze,'
In the next line it 'whispers through the trees.'
If crystal streams 'with pleasing murmurs creep,'
The reader's threatened (not in vain) with 'sleep.'

THAT most delighted in by ladies, and least appreciated by men, of all forms of active benevolence, a grand bazaar in aid of some local charity was to be held at Netherlaw, consequently the hands of every woman in the district were full. Moncrieff's hands were full—by proxy: she undertook all manner of fancy work, passed it over to Christian, and to herself appropriated the credit. When her friends congratulated her upon the tastefulness of productions which she had *not* produced, she equably—yes, and in Christian's very presence too!—accepted the praise. Nothing of that sort surprised Christian now ; nor did she even think it worth while to remonstrate.

'Wasn't it funny!' Moncrieff said ; 'for instance, Maryanne Kirkpatrick *would* insist upon knowing how I contrived the glove sachets. I said I had forgotten how ; then she wanted to see the copy, so I told her it was lost. She is always hunting after patterns and stitches. Such a bore of a girl! and *isn't* she plain ?'

Whether, on account of Moncrieff's absence or not, Dugald found the country very dull about this time ; and for some part of nearly every day they were sure of the pleasure of his company at Argyll Gardens. On Christian he had at first cast an unfavourable eye ; for, as he once observed to his sister, 'Pretty governesses and companions are fatal man-traps.'

'Is she pretty ?' Moncrieff had carelessly inquired.

'Pretty enough to put a man on guard,' he had rejoined, and had since been on guard accordingly.

Whenever he chanced to find himself in a room alone with Christian, he assumed the defensive. But the shield he selected was not taciturnity, it was reading. He would fetch a book and offer to entertain the young lady by reading aloud. Taciturnity would have served his purpose equally well, but reading suited his taste better, for he loved to read aloud; he believed he had a special gift that way: there Christian and he differed.

He had a gruff voice, which he himself believed to be organ-toned. When reading, he would draw out every stop, and fill the air with vibrations, which, by some absurd conjunction of ideas, invariably brought to Christian's mind the phrase, 'swellings of Jordan.' Mr Urquhart did not affect prose, but poetry only—poetry was much more soulful, he would say. It was no use for Christian to declare that she did not appreciate poetry. Such an assertion Mr Urquhart would not credit. Miss Elvester's taste might indeed be dormant; his, then, be the task of awakening it. But perhaps what they were at (he was on the threshold of Milton's Pandemonium when it came to this) might be too high-class for a commencement. Should they turn to the 'Idylls of the King?' But Christian looked fairly frightened at the idea of having to sit by while Mr Urquhart boomed through any of these.

'Not the Laureate either!' he exclaimed. 'Shall it be Pollock's "Course of Time," then?—But no, I think not; that is but a crude production, and lacks the magnificent roll of Milton's music. Ah, yes; here is something, Miss Elvester, which you ought to enjoy: "The Raven," by Edgar Allan Poe, a gifted young American. It is a fine effort of genius,—dirge-like, melodious.'

Christian informed Mr Urquhart that she already knew 'The Raven' by heart.

'Ay,' said he; 'but you may never have heard it read.'

She was obliged to admit that she never had, and as politeness would not allow her to say further, that she did not want to hear it read by him, she resigned herself, and during the following most sepulchral declamation, tried to think of something else. But 'The Raven' was not enough for Mr Urquhart that day. Attuning his voice to *adagio cantabile*, he now bore his unwilling listener on waves of resonance,

> 'Where Alph the sacred river ran,
>   Through caverns measureless to man,
>   Down to a sunless sea.'

How he revelled in—

> '. . . . that deep romantic chasm which slanted
>   Down the green hill athwart a cedarn cover !
>   A savage place ! as holy and enchanted
>   As e'er beneath a waning moon was haunted
>   By woman wailing for her demon lover ! '

Then how trippingly came—

> 'A damsel with a dulcimer
>   In a vision once I saw; '

(In the fulness of his heart Mr Urquhart pronounced it "saw'r"!)

> 'It was an Abyssinian maid,
> And on her dulcimer she played,
> Singing of Mount Abora . . .'

'Now that is what I call mellifluous,' said the reader when he had done; 'exquisitely cadenced and mellifluous.'

Christian did not say what she called it; but one of the loveliest fragments in the language was spoiled to her from that hour.

Though Christian had been pronounced 'pretty enough to put a man on guard,' she was one of those girls whose charm does not strike beholders all at once, but gradually steals over them; so it was some time before Mr Urquhart fully realised how greatly her golden brown hair became her—how beautiful was the curve of her milk-white throat—how beautifully sweet were the long-fringed, sea-blue eyes. Simultaneously with the full perception of such details was reached also the conviction that this pretty young governess was no man-trap after all, and that—well, in short, that she deserved to be married! She was fair, her ways were all pleasantly feminine—above everything, she would be easily moulded. This last consideration was of quite paramount importance; for, in Dugald Urquhart's estimate, a wife primarily consisted of so much material for a husband to mould. No suspicion crossed Christian's mind of there being these thoughts concerning her; only she more and more regarded Mr Urquhart as a weariness, and wished more and more fervently that he would try to make sure at what hour his relatives were to be found at home, instead of perpetually coming in just after they had gone out. But matters could not remain this way for ever; something must come of it. And something did come of it, which it now falls to relate.

One forenoon, Dugald having, for the twentieth time, arrived to find that his sisters, aunt, and cousin were off, did not send his name to Christian as in general, but unceremoniously proceeded to the back parlour where she sat.

'Ah, Miss Elvester, you are here!' he exclaimed, just as if it were a surprise to come upon her there. 'The rest are away to Mucklestanes, it seems. I have missed them again. Life runs in similitudes.'

Christian clearly remembered to have heard Mrs Cassillis mention the intended hour of departure to Mr Urquhart; she could but think, therefore, that the gentleman had a most leaky memory.

'Since I am here, I suppose I may as well remain,' said Mr Urquhart.

Willie Ruthven, who was forming a procession across the floor, of the tenants of a Noah's ark, and who found his kinsman of Craigie Urquhart an obstacle in the path, made bold to observe,—

'This is my Miss Elvester's room, and she doesn't want you here, cousin Dugald; get out, please.'

Cousin Dugald lavished no wealth of affection upon Willie: he held little boys and girls to be, on the whole, a mistake.

'You spoil that monkey among you, Miss Elvester,' he remarked.

'Forgive us it,' she answered, smiling; 'it is a way we have.'

'A child should be kept in his own place,' said Mr Urquhart, rather testily, and forgetful that in the present instance it was he and not the child who happened to be out of place.

Christian bade Willie ask his cousin's pardon for having spoken so rudely; and Willie, after considerable demur, yielded to say,—

'If you please, cousin Dugald, I apologise.'

Upon which Mr Urquhart seemed appeased, and, sitting down, watched Christian at her needle-work.

'What do you call that, Miss Elvester?' he would like to know after a while.

'I call it an apron,' she replied, holding up for better inspection the piece of green satin, round which she was sewing in coloured silks a wreath of variegated flowers.

'Very tasteful indeed,' pronounced Mr Urquhart.

'A little too gorgeous, perhaps,' she said,
'but it is for the bazaar, and Mrs Cassillis
tells me that over-colouring never comes
amiss in Netherlaw.'

'And what Mrs Cassillis tells her, Miss
Elvester swears to. Well, my aunt is rather
a superior woman.'

'Mrs Cassillis is as near as possible to
perfection,' said Christian warmly.

But Mr Urquhart did not care to hear
what Christian thought about Mrs Cassillis.
He always found it to be more blessed to
give than to receive information.

'Do you know what my ideal of woman-
hood is?' he asked.

'An Aurora Leigh, I should imagine,'
guessed Christian.

'No, Miss Elvester, no; there you mistake
me; nothing so horribly clever could I endure. A quiet, loving, domestic woman—
as feminine as she is fair: that is my ideal.'

'Must she be very quiet?' said Christian.

'Sufficiently so,' was the rather ambiguous
reply. 'We men exceedingly dislike any-

thing loud, or aggressive, or self-important, in your sex.   It is a mistake to suppose that we want women to be intellectual, or even clever.   There is enough of intellect, of cleverness, among ourselves.   What we seek and must find when we come to you is, a rest—a change.'

'This gets rather interesting,' said Christian to herself.   Then she continued aloud,—

'Even though we be clever, our cleverness is so different from yours that, if the rest be in change, you have it still.'

'Excuse me, but we want none of that sort of thing at all.   What end does it serve?   Some young ladies court notoriety by writing novels and the like, as if *they* were competent to deal with the problems of life!   But they waste their pains; for who reads such poor stuff?'

'Do not you, Mr Urquhart?'

'*I! Never*, Miss Elvester.'

'How, then, can you tell that it is poor stuff?'

Mr Urquhart passed over this question

as irrevelant, and did so with an air as if
Christian had said something excessively
silly ; but he, out of the benevolence of
his nature, would try to excuse her for this
time.

'Speaking of writing happens to remind
me,' he observed, in a careless, off-hand
style, that did not sit upon him well at all,
'that I have with me a short poem, which
you might like to hear.' (Christian shuddered.) 'It is by a friend of my own,
who would, I am sure, be glad to have
an unbiased opinion as to its merits.'

This seemed odd ; for Dugald bore a
sufficiently strong family likeness to Moncrieff, to make it matter of surprise that
he should feel so much interested in the
performance of any friend.

'No poet could care for such an opinion
as mine,' represented Christian, most anxious
to get off ; 'it isn't in the least worth
having.'

'You are a unit, and an aggregate of
units constitutes the great public,' replied

Mr Urquhart, speaking as if he were divulging a new discovery to mankind. 'The opinion of the public,' he added, 'must be of a certain importance to every writer.'

Then he got up, took a sheet of paper from his pocket-book, and began to pace the room. There was no help for Christian. With as good a grace as possible she might submit herself to circumstances.

'You will be perfectly candid, I hope,' said Mr Urquhart; 'you will express precisely what you feel.'

'But that might be awkward,' she objected. 'How can I say so, if my opinion of the poem should be as low as yours is of ladies' writings?'

The young person was really showing herself painfully flippant. But Mr Urquhart would forgive her this time also.

'Say whatever you think,' he returned. 'It is a short thing; it will not weary you. Its title is, "Beneath the Trysting Tree."'

And having thus premised, he unfolded his scroll, prepared his voice, and began sonorously :—

> ' We lingered 'neath the trysting tree,—
>   She youthful, I in manhood's prime ;
> Before us heaved the gurgling sea,
>   Unwrinkled by the touch of time.'

And so forth in like manner. The production was rather under than over the average merit of efforts fated to remain in manuscript ; and it was meant to be pathetic, but not having come from the writer's own heart, it was little likely to touch the heart of any other body. About midway through, the lover was telling his beloved the sorrowful news, that it would now be necessary that they two should wrench themselves asunder for all time, since, alas !—

> ' The forceful Fates have frowned on us,
>   Our high hopes they have trampled on,'—

when—

' Oh, cousin, you've been and broken the neck of my best giraffe !' interrupted Willie Ruthven, in shrill distress.

And sure enough cousin had, in suiting his
action to that of 'the forceful Fates,' unwit-
tingly planted his heel full on the head of
the ill-starred giraffe with disastrous results.
Still, it was altogether insufferable to be cut
short after such a fashion, and Mr Urquhart
frowned (without meaning to imitate 'the forceful Fates' this time), and angrily muttered,—

'Contemptible!'

Whoever or whatever aggravated him
always *was* contemptible.

'And he was my nicest giraffe,' lamented
poor Willie, with trembling lip, 'and I liked
him better than them all; but now he's
gone!'

Christian took the child on her lap, saying
soothingly,—

'He isn't gone, my pet; we'll have him
mended so that you could never know his
head had been off,—just as we had your cart-
horse mended, you remember.'

This assurance comforted Willie, and he
hastened to the floor again to gather together his scattered flock, and put them out

of further harm's way. Cousin Dugald the
while looked on in a state of extreme irrita-
tion, which nothing would so effectually have
relieved as just to take a tramp of destruc-
tion over the entire herd. But before we
condemn, we ought to consider how trying
it must have been for him to be wrested from
the very heights of Parnassus and confronted
with such a desperately prosaic fact as a child
whimpering over a broken toy.

But patience mends all. So, by-and-by,
the reading was resumed and carried on
without hindrance, till the parting lovers
were left with the consolatory hope that,
though sundered now, they should yet be
reunited,—

> ' Amid the viewless winds to dwell,—
> Ne'er, ne'er again, while ages roll,
> To sigh that saddest sound, Farewell !'

A pause. Mr Urquhart expected Christian to be complimentary, and complimentary
Christian could not conscientiously be.

'Well, Miss Elvester?' he said sugges-
tively, when he was tired waiting,—

'It—it—it goes quite smoothly,' was all that she could muster in reply.

'Of course—of course ; every line has the proper number of feet.   But the sentiment—what of the sentiment ? '

Again silence.   How could one speak so as at the same time to be truthful, and to avoid giving offence ?

'Do you '—it evidently cost Mr Urquhart an effort to conceive the possibility—' do you not like it, Miss Elvester ? '

'Oh, I haven't said that.'

'You have said nothing.   *Do* you like it ? '

'I don't dislike it.'

'There is no getting at your opinion ! What faults have you to find ? '

'Faults ?   I don't wish,—what right have I to find any faults ? '

'My dear Miss Elvester, is this your way of giving a candid opinion ? '

'Is it fair, Mr Urquhart, is it fair to cross-question me so ? '

'Perfectly ; the object being but to obtain an unambiguous reply.'

Driven into a corner, Christian saw nothing for it but to tell her mind.   First,—

' Are your friend's verses founded on fact ? ' she asked ; ' because if they are, I won't say one word.'

' The poem is drawn from fancy entirely,' responded Mr Urquhart.

' Then, if I must criticise, will you show it to me, please ? '

Instead of showing it to her he re-read it, as resoundingly as at first, but more slowly, that she might mark and consider every separate cadence ; which done, he once again requested to know what fault she could find.

' The "gurgling" sea—"gurgling" doesn't seem to be a very happy expression, does it ? ' she ventured.

' I consider it an exceedingly apt expression,' said Mr Urquhart, quickly, ' fresh and unhack- neyed. Have you never heard the sea gurgle ? '

' No ; but perhaps our Northern Ocean isn't civilised enough to gurgle, — it roars generally.'

'Ah,' rejoined Mr Urquhart, becoming very stiff; 'and what other amendments have you to suggest?'

'Have I not said enough?'

'Not so; say all you think—say all.'

Goaded on at this rate, Christian would say all.

'The line below "the gurgling sea" reminds one too much of a line in Byron's address to the ocean,' she proceeded. 'Then in the first line of the next stanza, your friend has "a sea of tears," which is surely a sea too many. Besides, I can't think that the lady's eyes, "raining a sea of tears," could at the same moment be fixed on his, as he says they were; one would hardly be able to "fix" one's eyes while tears flowed like that.'

'I beg your pardon,' said Mr Urquhart, coldly desperate; 'but this is the merest verbal criticism, and I flat—my friend flatters himself, that he quite understands what he is about. Kindly leave these quibbles, and be good enough to state how the poem strikes

you, viewed as a whole.   Make your remarks
without reservation.'

'Very well, if you *will* hear all, it is that
your friend's verses strike me as amateurish.
They want the ring of poetry written by one
who writes because the thing is in him and
he must.   They are much like what I have
sometimes seen in the " Poet's Corner" of the
Cornrigshire Chronicler.'

'Thank you—thank you!' exclaimed Mr
Urquhart, mortified past the power of concealing his mortification.   'You do assuredly
pronounce with great authority for a young
lady who lately professed to believe that her
opinion was of no value.'

'I believe so still,' said Christian, rather
taken aback; 'and but that you insisted, I
would not have given it.'

But black was the cloud that darkened
Dugald's brow as a second time he ironi-
cally thanked Christian for her obliging remarks upon his 'friend's poor lines;' and
bitter his smile as he quitted Argyll Gardens.   That was the girl whom he had

fancied ready to be as clay in the hands of the potter—that! Amateurish! The poet's corner of *The Cornrigshire Chronicler.* One thing, at any rate, was now a certainty— Christian Elvester should never be wife of his.

CHAPTER XIII.

AN ATALANTA RACE.

'Ah, Fear! ah, frantic Fear!
I see, I see thee near;
I know thy hurried step, thy haggard eye,
Like thee I start, like thee distracted fly.'

BOUT the end of December, Christian, who had hitherto declined all public amusements, got her first sight of fashionable Netherlaw in the mass. A singer of European fame was to appear at a concert in the Town Hall.

'It is but once in a while we provincials have so great an opportunity,' Mrs Cassillis said. 'I will accept no excuse. You ought to come with us, and you shall.'

So Christian went.

The Town Hall was in the heart of Netherlaw—shoved into an out-of-the-way corner, and jostled by the Vegetable Market on this hand, by the police-office on that; and, in order probably not to put these its neighbours out of countenance, it was the dingiest, ugliest Town Hall ever tolerated by wealthy townspeople.

On entering, Christian thought that the concert-room, with its various decorations, including printed notices hanging round, to inform the public that no smoking or standing upon seats would be allowed, was one huge sin against good taste. But very soon she lost sight of her surroundings. Listening to the famous singer, she felt as if she would be well content to continue there and thus for ever. That could not be, of course; at the end of two hours or so she had to rise and accompany the multitude from the concert-room. Dreamily and mechanically she went, for the music had powerfully affected her. It does not do, however, to

be dreaming in a crowd; and that Christian
proved, when she let go her companions, and
mistook the turning, and descended the
wrong stair, and only after considerable difficulty succeeded in making her way to the
cloak-room.

On arriving there, whom should she find
in waiting but Moncrieff, who had gone
home to Craigie Urquhart a week ago,
and had not been heard of since.

'How do you do? Hasn't it been such
a slow affair? I hate those ridiculous en-
cores. What an age that absurd creature
has kept you,' said Moncrieff, all in a
breath.

'I stupidly lost my way; no absurd
creature kept me,' replied Christian.

'Didn't she? Aunt Marjorie noticed a
Mrs Smilingly or something nodding and
waving her handkerchief to you; and she
thought you must have stayed behind to
speak to her.'

'Mrs Smillie? I never saw her, nor you
either.'

'We were behind you, and she was waving from the front of the balcony. Aunt Marjorie has gone down ; but she sent Glen to hunt you up, and left me to wait here till you should come, to tell you that you can't have a place in the carriage. Dugald and I are to go to Argyll Gardens to-night, of course, and there isn't room in the carriage for everybody, as Aunt Marjorie had offered a seat to Mr Fyfe Armstrong before she knew of Dugald and me. So Dugald has gone to bring a cab for you, and I am to go now with Aunt Marjorie. You must wait at the hall door, so that he can't miss you.'

This seemed to Christian a very singular arrangement, particularly the waiting at the hall door part of it. Why could not Mr Urquhart come to the cloak-room for her? That would surely be the more natural way. Hers not to reason why, however, so she merely said,—

'Very well,' and prepared to obey.

'How I shiver,' complained Moncrieff. 'I've not wrapped myself up half enough ;

and some one must have run away with
my hood. I can't find it anywhere. What
a delightfully comfortable wrap yours seems
to be, Miss Elvester.'

'I shouldn't wonder if she would take
it, and my hood, too,' thought Christian.
'I must try.'

'It is comfortable,' she answered. 'Won't
you have it, since you feel so cold?'

'Thanks very much. You are lucky in
never knowing what to feel cold is,' said
Moncrieff, drawing near as she spoke, that
the covering might be thrown over her.

'And my hood,' suggested Christian;
'won't you take that as well? I don't want
it myself any more than I want the wrap.'

'Don't you, indeed? Then, if you will be
so kind, I shall be glad of it, since my own
has been carried off by some stupid.'

So the hood was given to her also, and
she, in her borrowed gear, ran down to the
carriage with Captain Cassillis, whom she
encountered in one of the passages, and
satisfied as to the object of his quest.

Moncrieff's selfishness was so thoroughly ingenuous that it frequently, as in the present instance, provoked Christian into trying how far it would go. But Christian had better have refrained from the experiment to-night, for she felt need enough for her own coverings, when she took her stand at the hall door, and began to weary for the cab which Mr Urquhart was to bring. Minute after minute passed, each seeming longer than the one before, but still it did not come; all the people went away, and the hall was closed, and Christian was left alone—but still it did not come; the steeple-clock at the cross struck eleven—but still it did not come.

It was no time for a girl to be lingering here. So bitterly cold as it was too; and she bareheaded, and with nothing warmer over 'her evening dress than the lightest of opera cloaks. How she trembled, as she shrank closer to the hall door, under the awning; and even if she had not trembled with cold, she would have trembled

before long with fear.   Gradually the wonder
why Mr Urquhart was so tardy about fetching the cab, gave way to the conviction that
he did not intend fetching it at all.   What
could be the meaning of it?   Was ever
any girl in such a dismal plight?

And now were heard the shouting and
laughter of a too hilarious crew, turned
into the streets from the tavern by the
Forbes Mackenzie Act, but jubilantly resolved not to go home till morning, till
daylight did appear.   The sound came
nearer—nearer; the tramp of unsteady feet
advanced.

Christian would wait here no longer;
she dared not brave a gang of tipsy rev-
ellers; she must at all hazards do the best
she could to get to Argyll Gardens.   She
had not the faintest notion of the way; only
she might be fortunate enough to guess
aright.   Forth she came, then, and passed
fleetly along this narrow street into the wider
one beyond.

What a night it was!   The skies would

have been black, but that they were aglare
with the reflection of many furnaces, and
the rain was falling in the way Netherlaw
rain does fall, as if it would never leave off
again.　Not weather, assuredly, for a bare
head, gauzy dress, and satin shoes.　Still,
the deluge, if in one respect it incommoded
Christian, in another was of service to her;
since because of it the public ways were
deserted, and, excepting the boon companions she had fled from before, no living
thing was abroad either to wonder at or to
molest the girl; so at least for a time.　But
when she reached Arcade Street, the show
street of Netherlaw—through which she
must have driven ere now with Mrs Cassillis, though she certainly did not recognise
it again,—and while she hesitated, not knowing whether to go up that would bring
her right, or put her altogether wrong, a man
appeared from an opening opposite and,
catching sight of her, suddenly halted.　She
at once hurried on, and—and—she was sure
of it! the man crossed in pursuit.　To the

other side she ran. The man increased his
speed and followed, Her heart gave great
wild throbs of terror;—she sped on—up—
across; no matter whether right or wrong
now. Yet, though she almost flew, she
could still hear the pursuer's footsteps keeping fast behind. All the buildings here
were business premises, therefore empty
at this hour; so there was no refuge.
What would she do? What must become
of her?

Still rushing on, as if for dear life, she
at the last extremity descried help afar off
in the shape of a policeman turning a corner, and, thank Providence! he came in her
direction. He advanced with measured tread,
looking, as a matter of form, to the security
of each door he passed. At sight of the
flying girl's figure, he stopped short and
waited. He was witness of too many sen-
sational night-scenes to be easily stirred
from his stolidity. He did not even specu-
late; not he! unmoved, unwondering, he
was ready for anything that could betide.

When Christian got near enough for
speech, she gasped out,—

'I've lost my way. Tell me how I shall
reach Cassillis Gardens.'

'No such a place hereaway,' said the
policeman, and he turned the light of his
lantern full on the questioner's face—a very
frightened face, all wet with rain, and surrounded with dripping love-locks. The
garments of this unlucky one were dripping
too, and her white satin shoes were no
longer white, and altogether she was in a
pitiable case.

'I am a stranger in Netherlaw,' explained
Christian, speaking as well as she could for
panting—she saw that she was looked upon
as a suspicious character, nor could she
marvel at that. 'I got separated from my
party at the Town Hall to-night, and now I
can't find my way to Argyll Gardens.'

'That's a different tale,' responded the
policeman; 'you said Cassillis Gardens last
last time, miss.'

Then he gave the required directions;

through by Saint Barnabas, straight up
River Street as far as Lockerbie Street,
along Lockerbie Street to the Western
Cross—'

'I should know my way if I were at the
Western Cross,' said Christian, ' but I—'

She stopped, and scarcely knowing what
she did, grasped the policeman's arm for
protection.

'Don't you be feared,' said the giant reassuringly ; ' I'll soon settle *him ;*' and he
wheeled about to face the cause of this
pretty girl's alarm.

'What's the meaning of this, sir ?' he
demanded in tones of thunder.

'The young lady has made a mistake ;
that is all, my man,' replied the pursuer,
quite unabashed.

And *then* Christian knew that she had
this whole time been measuring her speed
with that of Captain Glen Cassillis.

CHAPTER XIV.

AUNT EUPHEMIA.

> The Dowager, in ancient flounces,
> With snuff and spectacles she folly trounces,
> And, moralising, thus the age denounces.

ON her return from the concert, Mrs Cassillis found visitors : Quentin of Baronshaugh, namely, and the dowager lady his mother. The Laird of Laighbield, though in his twenty-first year, looked the merest boy ; and he was a vague, limp lad, who would by no means have answered the requirements of a Mrs Baillie Geddes in respect of stamina.

What the poor Quentin lacked in individual colouring, his mother more than made up for. Behold her,—A tall, angular form,

with sharp features, small, dark, piercing
eyes, no lips to mention, and high cheek-
bones, abutted on by grey, stern, stiff comb-
curls. This was a woman who wore dresses
of a proper walking length, and who never
allowed her back and the back of chair,
church-pew or carriage even for one half-
minute to remain in contact, so upright she
was. She held gloomy views in regard to
the rising generation, — gloomier than all,
regarding her niece Moncrieff; Moncrieff
lounged; Moncrieff trailed yards of useless
material behind her when she walked; Moncrieff was wholly given up to vanity. The
dowager's salutation to this sad, young re-
lative of hers when they met in the drawing-
room at Argyll Gardens was,—

'From home again, Moncrieff! You do
not obey the apostolic injunction laid upon
women, to be keepers at home.'

'I have just been at home for a whole
week,' said Moncrieff righteously; 'and one
stagnates when one is more than a week
without seeing anybody, Aunt Euphemia.'

Being of the class who are constantly saying censorious things, and then taking credit
for their quite unnecessary candour, calling
it straightforward honesty, Aunt Euphemia
hereupon added to the apostolic injunction
her own opinion anent the subject of idle
gadders about, ranking them with tattlers
also, and busy-bodies, who speak things that
they ought not.

Moncrieff, it is to be feared, did not lay
the homily to heart as could have been
desired ; her attention wavered a good deal,
and on the first possible opportunity she
hastened to exchange the dowager's dreary
didactics for the more congenial attentions
of Quentin and Glen.

In process of time Dugald came in.   But,
strange to say, he came alone ; so the question at once arose, what of Miss Elvester ?
Mr Urquhart really could not say ; he had
never spoken to, never even thought about,
Miss Elvester to-night.

'You were to bring her up in a cab,' said
his sister ; ' I told you so.'

'Ah, so you did; it occurs to me now,' he rejoined, with a supreme air; 'but I told you in return that I would do nothing of the sort; that it was no affair of mine to look after my aunt's governess.'

'Well, Dugald, it was a very nasty thing to say; but, anyhow, I never heard you say it.'

'That must have been because you were listening to somebody else.'

'It must have been because you have such a hoarse voice. It was very disagreeable not to repeat, especially when I told Miss Elvester to wait for you at the hall door.'

Glen, who had been looking more and more surprised, threw down the shawl— Christian's shawl—which he had just taken from his cousin's shoulders, and broke in,—

'Told Miss Elvester to wait at the hall door? You said to me, when you left her in the cloak-room, that she would not come with us, preferring to wait and drive up with Dugald. Mother' (as that lady entered), 'there has been a misunderstanding, it seems ; Miss Elvester has been left behind.'

' Left behind !' echoed Mrs Cassillis. ' How has it happened ? '

' Moncrieff here will tell you how.'

' You know yourself there wasn't room for everybody in the carriage, Aunt Marjorie,' said Moncrieff, thinking it too bad that any responsibility should be thrown upon her.

' Miss Elvester, at any rate, would have found room.   But when I questioned you, Moncrieff, you distinctly gave me to understand that she had arranged to follow us immediately with Dugald.'

' I couldn't have said " arranged," ' Aunt Marjorie.'

' My dear child, you did say " arranged." I particularly remember it, because I did wonder a little that Miss Elvester should do anything so unlike herself as to make such an arrangement, without any reference to me.'

' It is all your doing,' said Moncrieff, shifting the blame to her brother ; 'and I'm

sure if Maryanne Kirkpatrick knew how
really unamiable you are at heart, she would
stop saying that the girl will be very fortunate who marries you. But there can't
be any fear about Miss Elvester, can there?
Lost children are always taken to the police-
office; so if she didn't know where to find
a cab-stand, she would only have to turn in
there and stop all night. I daresay they
would give her their most comfortable cell,
especially if she mentioned whose governess
she is.'

Not sharing his cousin's ease of mind
respecting Christian, Glen forestalled his
mother's charge by saying that he would
go to the Town Hall at once.

'Dugald also, surely,' said Mrs Cassillis.
'Miss Elvester may be trying to make her
way home, and in that case, by taking
separate routes, one or other of you will
find her most likely, in some intermediate
street.'

Whatever Mr Urquhart's private feelings
were, he could not decently refuse com-

pliance. At the same time, it required no extraordinary discrimination to perceive that he did not glow with any fiery ardour to sally forth to the succour of this damsel in distress. Chivalry was very well in romance; in real life Mr Urquhart loved above all things to make and to keep himself comfortable.

Till Glen and Dugald were gone, Aunt Euphemia sat silent, taking notes. And the result of her observations when expressed was,—

'Yes, yes, Marjorie; this is a very pretty story indeed.'

'It is,' replied her sister-in-law. 'Alone, and at midnight, outside the Town Hall—unfortunate child that she is!'

'Humph!' said Mrs Cassillis of Barons-haugh dryly; 'my own idea is that she's not so much of a child as you suppose. Miss Elvester must be a very foolish young lady, indeed, if she could imagine that you intended her to stay behind you, waiting for Dugald. No, no, Marjorie; she knew what would happen, trust me, and decided that it would be pleasanter to return with your son than in general company.'

The best way of answering many of this acute woman's theories was not to answer them at all. So the other lady looked about, with the intention of saying something more on the subject of the recent misunderstanding to Moncrieff. But Moncrieff had very wisely vanished.

Quentin still remained, though conversationally he was null, having fallen asleep. And he slept peacefully on, till the reverberating tones of his cousin Dugald first made him dream of an army composed of drummers, and then wakened him.

Mr Urquhart had been unsuccessful in the quest. He had been to the Town Hall, all round about it, up and down every adjacent street and alley—yet here they saw him, with nothing but damp clothes to show for his infinite pains. He could do no more. He gave the business up.

But even though he had felt eager to carry it on, it would have been all one, since the need for exertion had happily ceased : while he was yet speaking, his cousin brought Christian home. And Christian came to light wrapped in Glen's overcoat, which caused Quentin to observe, in a drowsy aside to Dugald,—

'You couldn't tell whether she's a boy or a girl, you know.'

And caused Quentin's mother to cough ominously : a young woman who could, under *any* circumstances, parade the streets in male attire, was a young woman about whose principles there was grave reason to stand in doubt.

'We had an Atalanta race of it,' said Glen, laughing at the recollection. 'Miss Elvester took me for a midnight assassin ; and she is as fleet of foot as a young roe— she would not let me come within speaking distance of her.'

'Atalanta's race was a somewhat different affair from yours, I take it,' said Mr Urquhart.

'Who is Atalanta?' inquired the young laird.

He fancied she might be, or have been, a race-horse.

'The less we say, or think, or know, about these foolish Pagan myths the better,' cried his mother, with decision.

Then she fixed her eyes upon Christian, who was being disencumbered of the greatcoat by Glen, and sympathised with by the other Mrs Cassillis.

'You have got yourself very wet, Miss Elvester,' said the lady of Baronshaugh; 'and I have no doubt you feel extremely uncomfortable. But do you mean to tell us that you actually believed it to be the intention of Mrs Cassillis that you should stay behind the party, and that outside the Town Hall, waiting for Mr Urquhart? At the hour of midnight, too!'

Put in this way, the thing did seem an incredibility. Yet Christian *had* believed it, and had acted up to her belief. Before

she could answer for herself, however, Glen
interposed, saying,—

'My aunt is joking, Miss Elvester ; she
has a great fund of Scotch humour.'

And his mother hurried Christian away,
for Aunt Euphemia was looking dangerous,
and one never knew to what strange
lengths she might carry her straightforward
honesty.

As she passed Mr Urquhart, who was
posed statuesquely beside a well-filled flower-
stand, and who looked down as from some
higher world upon the present proceedings,
Christian wanted to thank him for his ex-
ertions on her behalf, but nothing of the
sort would he allow.

'No thanks, Miss — ah — Elvester ; no
thanks to me' (he said it languidly, at
least as languidly as such a voice was
capable of saying it) ; 'I would have
taken the same trouble for *anybody.* There
is no obligation, I assure you.'

This disclaimer, while it caused Christian
to understand how very little she bulked

in Mr Urquhart's estimation, was so
highly relished by Aunt Euphemia that
the good lady several times over nodded
her approval, exactly as she was used
to nod in her Church's General Assembly
when a favourite divine made a telling
point.

No thanks fell to Captain Cassillis for his
share of the trouble : when he opened the door
for his mother and Christian, he and the latter
silently shook hands.   That very silence was
fraught with meaning in the eyes of Aunt
Euphemia.   Words could be weighed and
measured, but these significant silences, what
might they not cover?   If this soft-voiced,
blue - eyed Shetlander was to remain long
under the same roof as Glen Cassillis, why,
let Marjorie look to it.   Did young ladies of
fallen fortune enter households such as this
with no other end in view than merely the
winning of their bread?   Mrs Cassillis of
Baronshaugh trowed not;—Mrs Cassillis of
Baronshaugh knew better.

Of course she did.   It had always been

her specialty to know better and see farther
than any one else, and when she could not
possibly either see or know, she did the next
wisest thing, and suspected; for, well-versed
in Scripture as she was, her biblical studies
had certainly not included the 13th chapter
of St Paul's first Epistle to the Corinthians.
Yet one cannot doubt her righteousness; she
never doubted it herself.   She frequently
drew a parallel between her own case and
that of just Lot, who vexed his righteous
soul from day to day with the unlawful deeds
of the wicked; and was not her present
object in town to countenance a public
meeting called to protest against the running of a proposed Sunday train between
Netherlaw and the capital?

On the day after Christian's midnight ad-
venture, the doctor who was called in (for
a doctor had to be called) said something
ominous about fever.   This caused a disper-
sion.   Dugald and Moncrieff were scared
out of the house at once—the latter still
thinking it very ridiculous that everybody

should seem to blame *her* because Aunt
Marjorie's governess had happened to get
a drenching ! Willie Ruthven was dis-
patched to a place of safety, and Quentin
of Baronshaugh was sent by his mother
afar. As for herself, the dowager would
stay where she was till her purpose of protesting against Sabbath desecration were
accomplished, braving danger in the path of
duty as a sound-principled, rightly-regulated
Free Churchwoman should.

Notwithstanding medical prognostications,
Christian did not come to any harm ; nothing
befel her more serious than an influenza cold,
and in a day or two she was able to leave her
room.

' There is no chance of your running away
from me this time,' said Glen, when he saw
her on a couch by the parlour fire.

And then, in spite of her rather constrained
reply (she always was a little constrained with
Captain Cassillis, somehow), he sat down and
showed every intention of making himself
agreeable. He, like his cousin Dugald, had

taken some time fully to realise Christian's peculiar charm ; but now-a-days, he thought, what a very pretty creature she was,—not like Moncrieff, of course, flashing before men's eyes with an almost blinding beauty, but a flower-like little thing who, though she would never dazzle, must surely always please.

'It's a hard case,' he said to her, smiling, 'that you should have to spend Christmas in this nunnery fashion. Have you anything to read ?—anything interesting, like—' and he named the book she had had in her hand when he saw her for the first time.

'Thank you,' she replied, 'I have more to read than I can manage. But I did not read that, though I opened it,' she added proudly ; 'only I see no reason why I might not, if I had chosen.'

'Nor do I. Yet I am rather glad that you did not choose.'

'I don't know why you should be glad ; I don't know why a man should think badly of a girl for having only done something which he isn't one bit ashamed of having done himself!'

'I will tell you why. It is because men want to be able to think very much better of girls than they can think of themselves. We are sorry whenever you condescend to meet us on our own level.'

This brought to Christian's mind the speech,—

'What we seek and must find when we come to you is, a rest—a change.'

And a smile flickered in her eyes for a moment, then was gone.

Meanwhile Mrs Cassillis of Baronshaugh had heard the call of duty bidding her hither ; so at this juncture she marched solemnly into the parlour. She ignored the chair which her nephew offered her, and looked about for one sufficiently uncomfortable to find pleasure in ; but, looking in vain, she had to accept Glen's in the end. She did so under protest, observing that this was an age of self-indulgence indeed ; our very seats were constructed in such a fashion as

to foster habits of lounging and sloth. Her
glance was upon the couch as she spoke,
and Christian, feeling the reproof, raised
herself into a position as erect as anybody
could desire.

'That is right,' said Mrs Cassillis. 'There
is nothing like keeping up. Illness may
often be warded off by just refusing to
recognise it. Half of the disease we hear
about is really nothing else than indolence
and self-indulgence.'

'So you see, Miss Elvester, if you have
a sufficiently strong will, you needn't be
ill at all; and if you're only determined
enough about it you may live for ever, I
suppose,' said Glen.

But Aunt Euphemia indicated that this
was 'foolish talking and jesting, which are
not convenient.'

'Had you a satisfactory meeting last
night?' inquired Glen, a little while after,
not that he cared about the meeting, but
only to divert attention from the couch, for
his mother had come in and was making

Christian once more resume the posture of indolent self-indulgence.

'A capital meeting,' said his aunt emphatically. 'Did you not read the report of it?'

'No; I contented myself with the *Reflector's* remarks.'

'And scurrilously low remarks they are, Glen. The *Reflector's* position must indeed be weak, when it stoops to make use of such sorry weapons.'

'Yes; it is a mean advantage to take of your protestors, to ask them why, in their zeal for the Fourth Commandment, they trample under foot such more excellent precepts as "Let brotherly love continue." Though there was a squabble on the platform, it was cruel to mention it; we others have no business to take notice when doctors disagree.'

'Oh, fie! there was no disagreement worth the name. Reporters have a way of garbling accounts, which says little for the integrity either of themselves or of the

newspapers that employ them.   Here are
the facts of the case :   That able man, Dr
Doeg Sledgehammer, in lamenting Sabbath
desecration in England, went on to remark
that it had before now justly been observed
of Episcopalians, that their response after
the reading of the Fourth Commandment in
their churches would be, if they were con-
sistent, "Lord, have mercy upon us, for we
are resolved to break this law. "   Upon
this Mr Harpiscord, the incumbent of St
Timothy's, got up in a most unseemly spirit,
declaring "that he was an Englishman, and
was proud of it ; he was an Episcopalian to
the back-bone, and gloried in it," and so forth
—and so forth.   It was ill-judged in the
extreme, and it has given the enemy occasion
to rejoice.   But from such a quarter what
could we expect ?   Yet, why speak of prelacy,
when there is in our very midst a church in
which Erastianism is rampant ; where the
flocks are starved, or, worse still, poisoned ;
where, as a rule, the ministry are slothful
and lifeless ; dumb dogs, as the Scriptures

calls such hirelings—the loaves and fishes all that they desire.'

' Is Dr Brackenburn according to rule?' asked Glen, his aunt having paused to draw breath.

' Dr Brackenburn is latitudinarian,' replied the lady, with disdain.

' Does that mean that he allows people to have hot dinners on Sunday?'

' It means that his views are dangerous, unsound, and unscriptural, Glen. But, even putting errors in doctrine aside, what can be said for a man who, holding Dr Brackenburn's position, makes a giddy, spoilt, and pampered worldling his wife?'

' Well, what can be said but that he was very much in love with her?'

' Stuff and nonsense, young man! Matilda Cannisbay has two thousand a-year, and *there* lies her attraction. And naturally, she is aware of her own power. Never did a minister's wife act so arrogantly; but in fact Dr Brackenburn himself is little better

at times. One day lately, for example,
when I met him out-of-doors, and was
laying before him my conscientious reasons
for refusing to subscribe to his wife's soup
kitchen, or in any other way encourage her
so-called charities, also putting it to him,
as a preacher of the Word, whether a day
of fasting and humiliation throughout the
parish were not a likelier means of re-
lieving the Laighbield poor than any
number of humanly - devised soup kit-
chens; when I was urging this upon him,
I say, he unceremoniously cut me short,
and for what purpose, do you suppose?
Only that he might pass on to an old pauper
whom he saw waiting for him.   Now, I
maintain that a minister ought ever to bear
in mind the scriptural precept, " Honour to
whom honour is due."'

> ' For even in heaven it is quite plain,
>   As stars with different glory shine,
>   There shall be people poor and fine,
>   For perfect order there shall reign,
>   And one wouldn't like to go over the line,'

quoted Glen, from a poem just then on every drawing-room table in Netherlaw.

And Glen's mother now turned from petting Christian, to say a word for the accused.

'I have always particularly admired Dr Brackenburn just for his freedom from respect of person,' she observed. 'To me it is beautiful to see him in his parish, calling the little children by name, and asking the mothers all about sons and daughters who have left the home. My present sewing maid is a Laighbield girl, and that young woman is a staunch believer in the infallibility of Dr Brackenburn.'

'Do you hold yourself justified in the encouragement of such an exalting of the instrument?' demanded the lady of Baronshaugh.

'I would rather have young people hero-worshippers than not,' said the other, 'granted they choose their hero wisely.'

'The fear of man worketh a snare, Marjorie.'

'Pardon me, by hero-worship I only

mean that reverent admiration of the higher than himself, which is what one of our moralists calls the perfect human faculty in man.'

'Perfect!' echoed Mrs Cassillis of Baronshaugh, wilfully twisting the sense to suit her own purpose, 'perfect human faculty! I open a certain old-fashioned book, Marjorie, and there I read, "The heart is deceitful above all things, and desperately wicked."' Then without suffering a reply, she went back to finish the sum of Dr Brackenburn's transgressions.

'They had lately in Laighbield parish church a sermon — or what *they* name sermon; *I* name it otherwise—on gossiping : they go to get the gospel, and they get gossiping.'

'They needed such a sermon, I'll be bound,' cried Glen. 'Dare one hope anybody laid it to heart?'

'That is what Dr Brackenburn is pleased to call practical preaching,' proceeded this would-be tuner of the national pulpit. What

I term it is a secularising of the sacred calling
—a degrading of the preacher's office. But I
thoroughly fathomed the meaning of the said
discourse. Dr Brackenburn is aware how
his wife is spoken about, and his idea is,
to shut people's mouths by convincing his
hearers that gossip is sinful. Had he been
a man of genuine stuff, he would have
scorned the pitiful subterfuge. But if he
wants texts of that description, I can supply
a text to him ; even this : " So must their
wives be grave, not slanderers, sober, faith-
ful in all things." '

Mrs Cassillis of Argyll Gardens never
argued with her sister of Baronshaugh ; so
she let this interpretation pass unchallenged.
Glen spoke.

' How about your own parson's wife ? ' he
asked. ' She's all right, I suppose—up to
the mark in gravity — sober enough to
please ? '

' She is an estimable person enough in her
own way, I have no doubt,' replied Aunt
Euphemia, speaking as if this were a sore

subject with her. 'Mr M'Spur, when a student, got entangled with a girl in his then position; and afterwards, though he might have done much better, *very* much better, he married her.'

'I fail to see how he could do better than marry the woman he had engaged himself to,' said Glen.

'A clergyman's wife ought always to be a gentlewoman.'

'That is an interpolation; it is not in the original canon. My dear aunt, I am shocked at such morality; even I, latitudinarian as I am, have stricter notions about the nature of a promise than your creed, so ultra-orthodox, seems to require.'

'Most ridiculous, Glen; the boy's promise is often wisely broken by the man.'

'Hardly, I should think, when the breaking of it may be breaking a heart as well.'

Sentimental refinement of their order Aunt Euphemia did not understand; and she demanded with cold scorn, if Glen himself would be prepared to throw distinctions of

class to the four winds, and marry some
village maid.

'Yes; if I had pledged my word to it,'
he answered, laughing; 'and though you
might refuse to acknowledge the bride, my
mother would be gracious to her, I think.'

With that Captain Cassillis withdrew, and
went to spend the evening at his club; he
could never manage more than half-an-hour
at a measure of Aunt Euphemia. Mrs Cassillis of Baronshaugh thought it a bad sign
in a young man, that he could not sit quietly
with his female relatives at home; so she
shook her head after the retreating form.

'I fear, Marjorie,' she said, 'that your son
has not been improved by a military life;
and I know he imbibed reckless, unsettled
notions while he lived about the Continent.
Germany is a very hotbed of Socialism and
its accompaniments. As to the universities,
they are nationalistic to the core; no student
who enters them escapes the taint. There
is that young man they have got in Auchterbrechan now, for example. He, not con-

tent with the ordinary curriculum, must, in
his pride of intellect, have a course of German theology, forsooth! So to Germany he
went.   Well; what is the consequence?
Simply this: his laxity of doctrine is such,
that had he belonged to the Free Church,
he would have been arraigned before our
higher court, and effectually silenced. But
in the State Church, where such as he fitly
take shelter, heresy may come in like a flood,
yet none seeks to stem the torrent.   I am
told that the said individual has the pre-
sumption to treat the inspired narratives as
if they were mere ordinary human composi-
tion, calling the story of Isaac and Rebecca
a quaint pastoral, if you please! and deny-
ing that Solomon was the author of Eccle-
siastes, and more of such profanity than I
can bring myself even to repeat.   By the
way, Miss Elvester, you must know the man
I mean.   I suppose you have heard that
he is a fortune-hunter like the rest of his
class.   No?   Well, now I tell you of it.
He is engaged to the niece and presumptive

heiress of Greatfellow, the rich bonnet manu-facturer. I *hope* the match may not yet be rued by all the parties concerned,' added Aunt Euphemia—with ' but I *know* it will be,' understood.

CHAPTER XV.

VEXATIOUS!

Oh, why should fate sic pleasure have
Life's dearest bands untwining?
Or why sae sweet a flower as love
Depend on Fortune's shining?

THE bazaar for which Christian had worked as Moncrieff's proxy was opened with demonstration, and carried on with energy; and those engaged in the gay fancy fair had all the satisfaction of at the same time enjoying themselves and advancing a good cause. It must be confessed that the former consideration only had any weight with Moncrieff. It was a pleasant thought, that of figuring among a garden of girls, herself conspicuously the

belle. And for a very little while the actual
fact was rather pleasant too. But as anybody who knew Miss Urquhart might have
expected, the edge of the enjoyment soon
wore off. The sale was to last five days :
by the end of the first the pleasure had
begun to pall; by the end of the second
Moncrieff had thrown the business up. The
heat and confinement had been 'too disgust-
ingly tiresome' to her. Worse even than
that, her colleagues had behaved in the most
atrocious manner; had actually objected to
her general method of procedure. For it
had not commended itself to them that Miss
Urquhart should systematically attend to
gentlemen customers only, and leave lady
customers to chance; or that she should
carry matters as though there was nobody
so much as to be thought of except herself :
her characteristic ignoring of all claims but
her own did not amuse these young ladies,
as it sometimes amused Christian. They
were, with one exception, justly indignant,
and made no scruple of letting Moncrieff

see that they were so. This exception was
the fancy-pattern loving Miss Kirkpatrick;
and she, whatever her secret thoughts might
be, spoke only words as smooth as butter to
Miss Urquhart. The other stall-holders
believed that they had the key to this; and
they smiled among themselves when Miss
Kirkpatrick entreated Miss Urquhart not to
forsake the flowers—for it was the flower-stall
at which these young ladies officiated—they
would wither and die if she did. But Moncrieff
was not to be won back by this pathetic remon-
strance; she washed her hands of the whole
affair, and drove off in a pet to Argyll Gardens.

They had told her that if she did persist
in leaving them, she must find a substitute—
so she at once got hold of Christian, and
unfolded all her woes.

'Of course, Miss Elvester,' she concluded,
'you will be the substitute.'

'I don't see that it is of course at all,' was
the reply. 'My sisters expect me at Laighbield this week; besides, I shouldn't know
how to be a saleswoman.'

Of the first objection Moncrieff took not the slightest notice. The expectations of Miss Elvester's sisters could be disappointed, and no harm done. One week was as good as another for Laighbield.

'You'll have no trouble,' she answered; 'you needn't give any change back. And you can ask what price you like for the flowers. Cousin Glen offered me ten guineas for a rose that I wore in my dress; but he wouldn't have given any one else so much, of course.'

'I suppose not.'

'You can have some cigars by you,' proceeded Moncrieff; 'men will pay anything you choose, if you've bitten off the ends. I wouldn't do such a sickening thing myself; but you can, if you care.'

'I don't think I shall care.'

'Oh! I daresay you will, if you can get enough money. But I wish I had never gone to these bazaars; I wish there was no such thing as a bazaar; as Dugald says, you get mingled up with such offensive people.

Now, Miss Elvester, *hasn't* it been vexatious to me ?'

Vexatious to her as it had been,—a vexation of a much more serious character followed close in its wake.   Christian agreed, out of pure good nature, to be the substitute ; so that was settled.   But Moncrieff could not be at ease till she had told the whole story to everybody whom she came near, and asked them separately and individually if they did not think it *had* been vexatious to her.

When Glen, in his turn, was appealed to, he did not show quite so much sympathy as might have been looked for.

'If it has been so vexatious to you, what is it to be to Miss Elvester ?' he would like to know.

Willie Ruthven, playing about the room, ran forward when this was asked.

'My Miss Elvester has gone to keep a bazaar,' he said, full of the subject.   'And grandmamma has gone with her too.   And I'm to be allowed to stay here for a while beside cousin Moncrieff,—I am.'

'Well, see that you don't make yourself troublesome, that's all,' said Glen. 'Cousin Moncrieff won't stand any nonsense, I can tell you.'

Something caught Willie's attention,—the child gazed at the man with round innocent eyes for a moment, then he asked,—

'Is the flower you've got in your coat the one you gave cousin Moncrieff ten guineas for?'

His uncle stared at him.

'Cousin Moncrieff said that you asked her to give you her flower from her neck for ten guineas, Uncle Glen.'

Moncrieff, with unwonted energy, sprang up, and herself rang for the nurse.

'I was doing a long, long sum on my new slate,' pursued Willie; 'and it was then that cousin Moncrieff came in. And I've got a whole guinea of my own, and ten fingers, so that is how I could keep so good mind about the ten guineas. And do you know what they do at bazaars too, Uncle Glen? they have cigars—cousin Moncrieff took a box of cigars from your room, nurse says so, and—'

Here fate in the form of 'nurse' seized upon Willie, and he was borne off struggling, and declaring that he would tell his Miss Elvester as soon as she came home; he would—he would—he would.

'That horrid little thing is quite idiotic,' observed Moncrieff, peace having once more settled down; 'you can't believe a word he says—so sinful? What is the use of Miss Elvester, if she can't teach him anything but story-telling?'

'The use of Miss Elvester,' rejoined Glen, satirically, 'is to go on with work that Miss Urquhart has undertaken, and got tired of.'

'Indeed, she was only too glad to have an excuse given her for staying on here, as long as *you* remain in Netherlaw: of course she was, cousin Glen.'

'For heaven's sake, Moncrieff, don't get into the way of saying such things. You can't know how they sound.'

'Oh, well, you can scold Dugald, for it was he who put it into my head. He says—'

'I won't hear what he says, not one word of it, Moncrieff; but if it was anything of that sort, he never in his life talked more absolute nonsense. But what about that ten-guinea offer of mine, that Willie tells us of? When did I offer you ten guineas for a flower?'

'You *would* have done it, if you had thought, cousin Glen.'

'But as I didn't think, why did you say I did do it?'

'I'm sure it's anything but nice to show yourself so inquisitive; indeed, it is quite old-maidish to be so prying and sly and curious.'

'Old-maidish let it be; but answer my question, please.'

'I quite detest to be questioned. It's very unkind of you. But if you must know, I said it just to keep up your credit.'

'How very considerate of you!'

'How very quarrelsome you have grown, cousin Glen. And men who are nice always do those things at bazaars.'

'More's the pity, I think.'

'It is all for the poor,' said charitable
Moncrieff; so I don't think you need grudge
it so much.   And at any rate, you *didn't*
give it; you didn't even buy a pair of gloves
or a flask of scent.'

'I am a mean beggar; but it can't be
helped.'

'It was a horrible bazaar, of course; still,
there were quantities of very useful things—
the sweetest fans and hair ornaments and
girdles.   I daresay you couldn't afford it,
cousin Glen.   But you could have borrowed
money, couldn't you?'

'From Dugald, for instance.'

'No; Dugald is parsimonious; he never
lends.   But there are money-lending offices,
aren't there—Three Golden Balls, or Bells,
or something.   At any rate, you might have
bought something, so that you mightn't have
been called penurious.'

'Penurious, did you say?   Well, it was
chill penury that repressed my natural desire
to stand high in your opinion and froze the
genial current of my soul.   Yet, I did buy

a trifle or two which I hope you will deign to wear for my sake.'

The attention was accepted quite as a matter of course, with a cool,—

' Thanks so much, cousin Glen.'

Moncrieff then went back to the borrowing idea.

' Why, if you are hard up, don't you raise money on your prospects ? ' she inquired. ' You will be so outrageously rich, you know, when your old bachelor uncle dies.'

' I have no bachelor uncle,' replied Glen. ' I have learnt to-day that my uncle contracted a private marriage years ago with a woman in a different station of life, and that he has now acknowledged his wife and family. Quite right of him, too ; only, there is an end to my prospects.'

Moncrieff was confounded ; she had always looked upon Glen as the undoubted heir to untold wealth.

' Oh, wasn't it low of him ! ' she ejaculated. ' And he nearly two hundred, the disagreeable old mummy !'

' He wasn't more than one hundred when he married,' said Glen ; 'and my mother's brother is a far finer-looking man than I am ; he cannot exactly be called a mummy.'

' I wish old men weren't allowed to marry,' cried Moncrieff. ' It puts one out so. There is a farce called " The Wicked World," but it isn't a farce, it is true, when old men are allowed to marry. Aren't you very furious, cousin Glen ? '

' Don't I look furious ? But never mind. I haven't lost all that makes life beautiful ; I have still my cousin Moncrieff.'

And so Glen turned off the thing with a jest. Nobody ever heard him adopt any other tone. If he did take the disappointment to heart, he certainly managed to cover his chagrin most effectually.

It was Moncrieff who harped on the pity of it, and wished that private marriages did not count ; and made out her cousin's uncle to be a hoary monster of iniquity. Yet, let it not be supposed that Moncrieff was for once making an attempt to forget self, and

bear another's burden. As a matter of fact,
nothing was farther from her mind. Among
the multitude of her admirers—or supposed
admirers, for on this subject the beauty
imagined a good deal—there was not one
whom she liked so well as Glen Cassillis.
It would be a mistake to say that she was
in love with him ; Moncrieff was incapable
of a passion ; yet she came as near to loving Glen as it was possible for her to come.
She had always intended to share Glen's
fortune. Nothing had been spoken between
them about marriage, it is true, nor did she
desire that there should be any verbal
agreement about the matter just yet. Once
engaged to Glen, he would insist upon re-
taining all one's favours to himself ; and
how particularly poky one would have to be.
So, freedom from the present, and flirtation
to one's heart's content ; then, at the proper
time, Glen would speak out,—Moncrieff had
not a doubt of it,—and everything would
come round exactly as one had planned.
And now to be suddenly informed that there

would never be any fortune for Glen at all. How cruelly disappointing! This was a vexation before which every other paled. Yes; it was a wicked world in which such misdemeanours as private marriages could be permitted—a wicked world, indeed.

Of course a marriage with Glen was now out of the question. Trying as it was to abandon that hope, it must be done. Glen was deposed accordingly, and Quentin set up in his stead.

Quentin's readiness to marry her was, Moncrieff believed, quite equal to Glen's; and Quentin seemed, on the whole, more eligible than any of the other men who were dying for her; his social standing was unexceptionable, and his estate brought him many thousands a-year. The one drawback—Aunt Euphemia—could be got over, by being disposed of in the distant dower-house, and never invited to Baronshaugh at all to worry one. (If Aunt Euphemia could have divined the imaginations of Moncrieff's heart!)

In the meantime, Glen must know nothing
of this to make him unkind and sulky. No
more presents from him, if he should discover how he had been forsaken. And that
would be a loss ; for Glen was not really
stingy, though one might call him so, just to
tease him a little. Poor cousin Glen! one
could not marry him, as bad fortune would
have it ; no, but one must as long as possible
keep on good terms with him.

So during the remainder of Glen's stay at
Netherlaw, Moncrieff's manner to him was
more affectionate than it had ever been
before.

END OF VOL. I.

COLSTON AND SON, PRINTERS, EDINBURGH.

www.ingramcontent.com/pod-product-compliance
Lightning Source LLC
Chambersburg PA
CBHW020853270326
41928CB00006B/679